AMERICAN GLASS
MASTERS OF THE ART

Lloyd E. Herman

Smithsonian Institution Traveling Exhibition Service
Washington, D.C.
in association with
University of Washington Press
Seattle and London

Published on the occasion of the exhibition:

American Glass: Masters of the Art

Organized and curated by Lloyd E. Herman

Circulated by the Smithsonian Institution Traveling Exhibition Service

Supported in part by the U.S. Information Agency

Printed and bound in the Philippines.

Distributed by the University of Washington Press, P.O. Box 50096, Seattle, WA 98145-5096.

Table of Contents

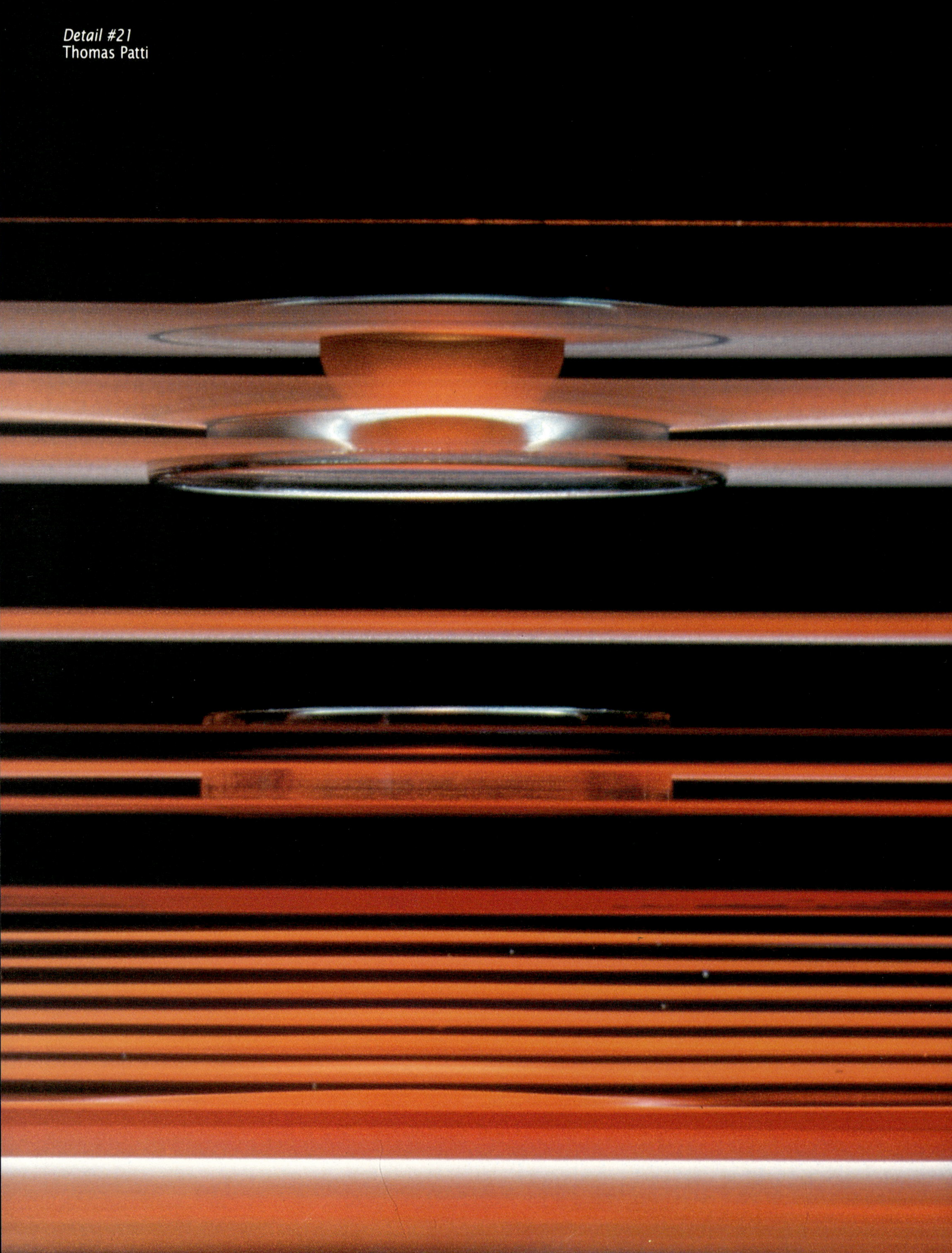

Detail #21
Thomas Patti

Preface

In the United States in the last thirty years, glass has emerged as a vital component of America's visual arts. In the Puget Sound region—with Seattle, Washington, at its center—there are an estimated 200 glass studios. Glass, basically sand melted to a liquid with the consistency of honey, can be blown into fragile bubbles, cast into sculptural architectural components, fused, painted, carved, and engraved, to name only a few techniques in the glass artist's vocabulary.

Glass is not an easy material to master if one wishes to form it. The sheer weight of a "gather" of glass at the end of a steel blowpipe necessitates the physical strength of the artist, or the careful and expert assistance of other skilled practitioners, to turn the glass into art. Nor is it an inexpensive medium in which to work. Unlike drawing, which requires only a clean piece of paper and a bit of charcoal, blowing or casting glass requires furnaces in which to melt it, annealers in which to cool it, specialized tools, and extraordinary amounts of propane gas to keep the furnaces operating. The artist must make either a volume of similar objects, or a few extraordinary, unique ones to sustain the expense of operating a hot-glass studio.

In the United States, glass sculpture may be found alongside paintings in the prestigious art galleries of New York, Chicago, Dallas, San Francisco, and other cities. It may be seen, too, in galleries devoted exclusively to art in glass. Increasingly, artists working in a sculptural style using glass cast in molds are awarded architectural commissions, rivaling their counterparts in the tradition of stained and leaded glass windows. An artist working in glass, Dale Chihuly, is only one of four Americans ever to have a solo exhibition at the Louvre. It looks like glass art is here to stay.

American art in glass did not develop on its own, in a vacuum. This survey includes recent examples of art in glass by thirteen artists selected from more than a thousand in the United States. It attests, however, to the heritage from Europe that American glassworkers acknowledge—for sources of style and technology and for the generosity in sharing information that marks the international glass art community today.

I wish to acknowledge the generosity of the artists, their galleries, and the collectors who have agreed to live without favorite art objects during this tour.

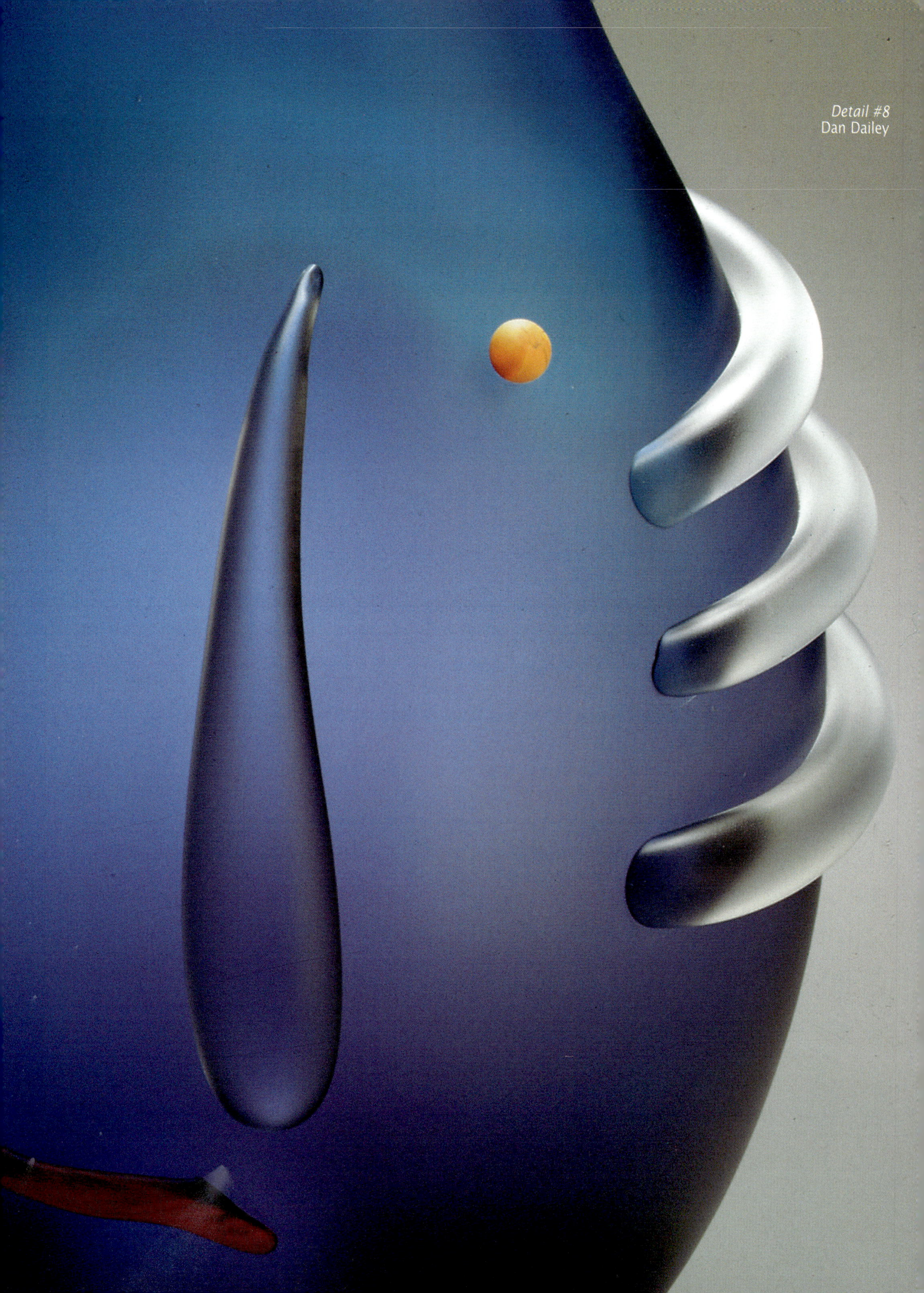

Detail #8
Dan Dailey

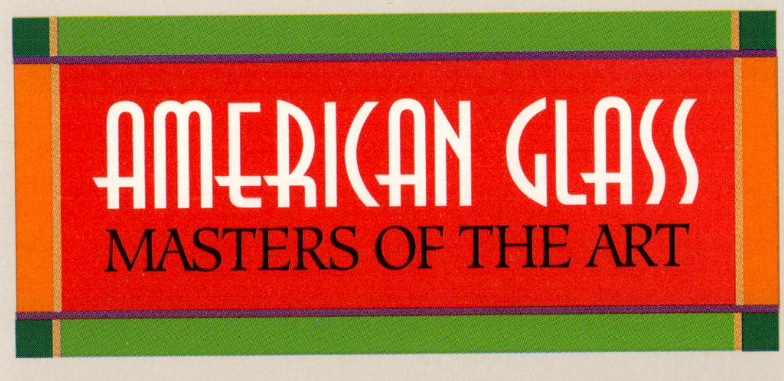

Glass is one of the world's oldest materials for art and, in America, one of the newest. Its aesthetic properties were recognized in Egypt and Mesopotamia as early as the second millennium B.C. Medieval stained glass windows in European cathedrals continue to awe visitors with their beauty and remind them of the long history of glass in art.

A century ago in the United States, glass factories were producing a variety of beautiful functional objects, but the concept of art made from glass was new. By the early 1900s two rivals, American-born Louis Comfort Tiffany and British-born Frederick Carder, were designing luxurious art glass that was made by skilled technicians in American factories. Tiffany became famous for his unique floral designs for leaded glass windows and lampshades and for the vases, desk sets, and other decorative accessories produced in his studios that helped to define the American manifestation of art nouveau. Carder was fascinated by the history of glass; his discovery of the techniques used in the past to manipulate it into beautiful objects brought success to his company. As founder of the Steuben Glass Works (now a division of Corning Glass Works, Corning, New York) and for the nearly sixty years he worked there, he supplied the wealthy and a growing American middle class with opulent vases, candlesticks, figurines, and dinnerware. The company continues to lead in the manufacture of crystalline tableware and small sculpture.

Other American companies specialized in producing cut glass crystal in the European tradition and pressed glass of varying quality, and have continued to do so to the present. Individual artists who wished to use glass as their medium had no way to melt and blow it in their studios, however. They had to find other ways to use the material. Clear or colored sheet glass could be composed into leaded glass pictures so familiar in church windows. Or it could be heated in a small kiln until soft, then formed into shallow bowls or fused in patterns onto other sheet glass. It could be decorated with fired-on enamel, itself colored glass ground to fine powder. It could be engraved, faceted, sandblasted, and painted.

Several American artists developed individual styles and processes in the 1950s. Michael and Frances Higgins in Illinois gained recognition in the 1950s for their fused glass serving pieces and giftware, as did Maurice Heaton in New York State for enameled decoration on factory-made glass dishes. In Ohio, Edris Eckhardt relied on her knowledge of ceramic glaze technology to develop her own methods of working glass. She formulated her own glass sheet or cullet, using a ceramics kiln and progressed to working glass sculpturally, using the *cire perdue* technique in which crushed glass fills a mold and is heated until it fuses. When it cools, the resulting sculpture is removed.

However, unique blown glass objects made by artists for creative expression have gained prominence only in the last thirty years. The breakthrough came in 1962 when Harvey K. Littleton, an associate professor of ceramics at the University of Wisconsin, and Dominick Labino, vice president and director of research at Johns-Manville Glass Fiber Corporation, organized two experimental glass workshops at the Toledo (Ohio) Museum of Art.

Littleton, whose father had been employed at the Corning Glass Works as vice president and director of research, saw in glass a new artistic opportunity. Labino, an inventor and glass chemist—and an active member of the Toledo Area Artist Group—provided technical expertise, bringing glass marbles that would melt at the temperature achieved by the small furnace they developed together. In the fall following those workshops, Littleton founded the first university glass program in the United States, at the University of Wisconsin. His lectures and film presentations on blowing glass stimulated development of glass teaching programs in art schools and universities in other parts of the country.

The most important glassblowing demonstration that Littleton and Labino participated in occurred at the World Crafts Council Congress in New York City in 1964. Labino's innovative furnace—taken to the conference for participants to see—was eventually copied by new glass programs in several schools, further expanding the opportunity for individual work in glass.

Dale Chihuly, a 1965 graduate of the University of Washington (where he had experimented with weaving glass strips into "window tapestries" as an interior design student), enrolled in Littleton's program. After graduating there and earning a second master's degree at Rhode Island School of Design in 1968, he was awarded a Tiffany Foundation grant and a Fulbright fellowship to study glass in Italy—the first American glassblower to study in Venice. His exposure to teams of skilled technicians creating glass designs would influence his later work.

Chihuly was not the only American influenced by European glass in the 1960s. Richard Marquis and Marvin Lipofsky had visited Italian glass workshops on the Venetian island,

Murano, in the 1960s, and Marquis has continued to employ and refine his use of Italian techniques in his own work.

There were other American introductions to European techniques and methods of working: Harvey Littleton at the University of Wisconsin, and Joel Philip Myers at Illinois State University both brought international glass artists to teach workshops in their glass programs. Lipofsky, hosting the Great California Glass Symposia at the University of California, Berkeley, and eventually at the California College of Arts and Crafts, from 1968 until 1986, also brought international glass artists to the United States.

"Europeans had the techniques, but Americans had the ideas. Each learned from the other," recalls Klaus Moje, the German-born artist who came to the United States in 1979 to teach at the Pilchuck Glass School in Washington State. Pilchuck quickly established itself as an international center for art education in glass after it was established in 1971; its summer programs continue to attract both faculty and students from many countries.

Today, university and summer glass programs in art schools continue the creative and technical communication developed first in the 1960s. Blown glass, once dominant, now is only one technique used by artists to realize a creative vision. Simply blowing a bubble of molten glass and turning it into a goblet, vase, or bowl is no longer enough. This survey includes monumental glass jars with elaborately decorated surfaces by William Morris—celebrated as one of the finest gaffers (master glassblowers) in the United States. Topped with meticulously crafted glass animal heads, they recall Egyptian canopic jars which held entrails for burial.

Richard Marquis is the American master of *murrine*—tiny designs incorporated along the length of slender glass rods. Though not alone in the United States in his use of *zanfirico (latticinio* in England and America) filigree of glass threads embedded in blown glass vessels, he personifies mastery of this technique also.

Dale Chihuly, after losing the sight of one eye in an automobile accident, adopted the European practice of directing a team of skilled gaffers to realize his glass visions. Of several extravagantly colorful bodies of work in glass, his "Venetians" are his own bold salute to Italian art deco glass of the 1920s, exaggerated to a grandly operatic scale.

Dan Dailey's blown glass faces often bring a smile to those who view them. He is adept at depicting an emotion by adding a stroke of molten glass to form a crooked eyebrow or a smirking mouth.

Michael Glancy relies on blown glass vessels, on the thick walls of which he makes patterns that are deeply sculpted by sandblasting, then partially electroplated with gleaming metal. The glowing color of light shining through the resulting "windows" gives his stately vessels the opulence of jewelry.

All of the artists whose work is shown here rely on color as an essential component of their creativity. Though Cappy Thompson paints her colorful narratives on colorless blown glass vessels, she does not blow glass herself. Instead, she relies on skilled gaffers—artists in their own right—to blow the classic vase forms that are her "canvas." Her paints are glass and metal oxides, applied with a brush, then fired under high temperature to fuse them to the vessel's surface.

Other artists use time-honored techniques other than blowing. Some have developed their own methods.

Both Paul Stankard and Ginny Ruffner rely on flameworking (lampworking), in which rods or tubes of laboratory glass are softened over a flame for manipulation. Stankard continues a long tradition of detailed botanical miniatures rendered in colored glass, encapsulated in hemispheres or plinths of clear glass. His work is revered especially by art collectors who prize elaborately detailed glass paperweights. Ruffner takes a bolder, sculptural approach to flameworking. Her assistants help to develop her designs in clear glass and assist in painting their surfaces to animate them.

Mary Ann "Toots" Zynsky "paints" with layers of colored glass threads. Extruded from a machine developed especially for her, her glass "spaghetti" is layered and fused into glowing bowls.

Like Zynsky, Thomas Patti has developed his own glassworking process, called "blown lamination," fusing layers of glass—some lined with color—into a block, then carefully injecting a bubble of air, which he expands into the solid interior. He uses color sparingly but, manipulating the optical qualities of glass, allows it into the viewer's perception from various angles.

Judith Schaechter brings her painter's eye for graphic imagery to the thousand-year-old tradition of stained glass. Her imagery, though, is clearly of the present. Adept at drawing as well as painting, her dark visions of contemporary life contrast with the brilliant colors of her palette.

Therman Statom also paints on glass, his vigorous brushstrokes defining the sheet glass walls of his constructed houses. His enigmatic narrative tableaux are given elusive meaning by his inclusion of "found" objects and loosely painted images.

Just as an artist's palette may hold many colors, today glass is often only one material in an artist's toolbox. Susan Stinsmuehlen-Amend once worked exclusively in glass, composing abstracted designs from commercial colored glass for windows, folding screens, and other architectural commissions. Now, like Statom, she uses glass in combination with other materials, creating three-dimensional "mixed-media" art.

Glass has become an international language in art. Americans design products for European glass factories, and artists from around the globe show their art in American galleries and teach or study at popular summer programs of the Pilchuck Glass School near Seattle. Museum exhibitions of glass, often traveling to multiple venues, and publications on glass art and artists help to satisfy the public interest in the magical material.

The styles of these artists' glass creations are as diverse as their techniques and, like art in any period, undeniably refer to the present as well as the past. Unlike artists even a century ago, those today rarely work in isolation. Indeed, contemporary artists are bombarded with visual information daily: advertisements, television and movies, fashion on the street, architecture, automobiles, electric signs. Even music, theater and dance can influence the visual arts.

In the early years of the American studio glass movement, the newest trend in American visual arts was pop art. Artists experimenting in glass as an art medium, like those sculpting clay, were undeniably influenced by banal commercial images: not only soup cans but telephones, political symbols, and other popular imagery beyond the limits of traditional art subjects.

This examination of recent American glass art is intended to demonstrate that American artists working in the medium follow no single trend or tradition but draw freely from the world and its visual history. Whether their art takes inspiration from Egyptian canopic jars, medieval stained glass windows, Venetian glass techniques, or Italian style, American artists working in glass use the world for their sketchbooks and are masters of their art.

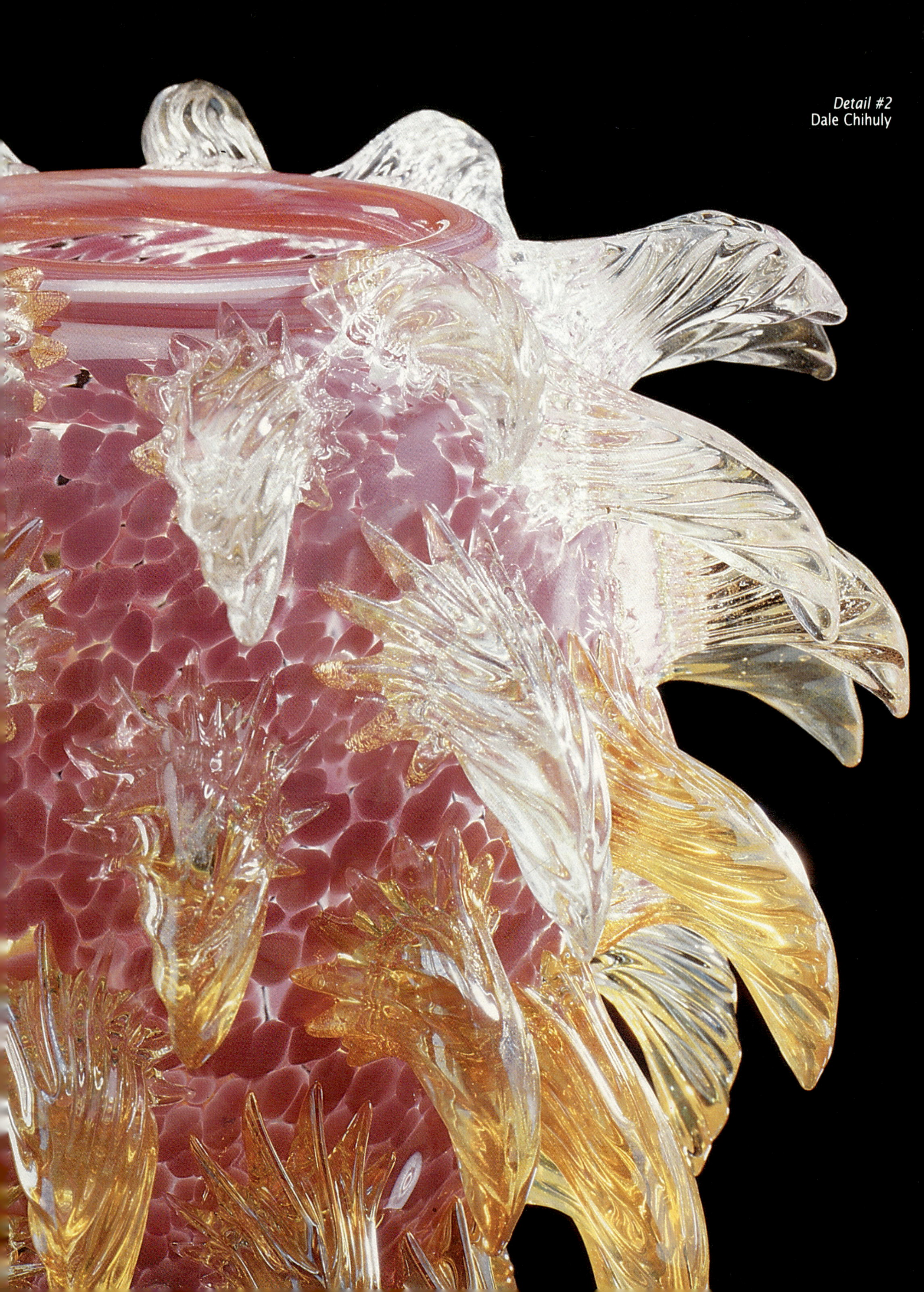

Detail #2
Dale Chihuly

AMERICAN GLASS
MASTERS OF THE ART

THE ARTISTS AND THEIR WORK

All dimensions are in centimeters. Height precedes width, precedes depth.

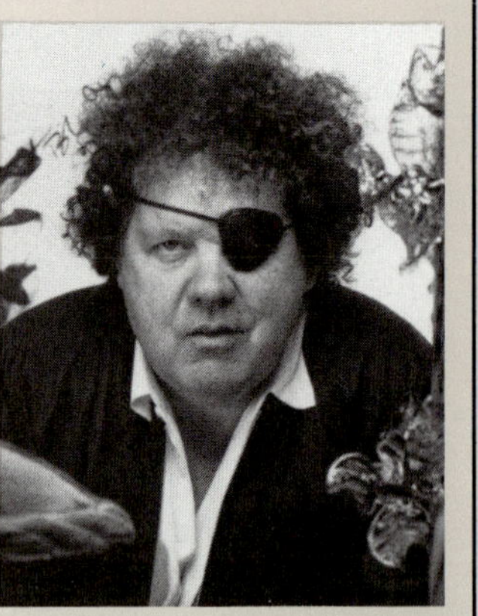

Kim Zumwalt photograph, 1989

DALE CHIHULY

Dale Chihuly, more than any other artist in the United States, has brought the medium of glass in art to public attention. One of only four American artists ever to have had a solo exhibition at the Musée des Arts Décoratifs, Palais du Louvre, in Paris, Chihuly is represented by glass art in museums worldwide. After earning a master of fine arts degree from Rhode Island School of Design in 1968, he was awarded grants to study glass in Italy and was the first American glassblower to study in Venice. There he observed the team approach to creating glass art that he adopted later, when the loss of sight in one eye forced him to stop blowing glass himself.

He also furthered education in glass art when in 1971 he cofounded the Pilchuck Glass School near Stanwood, Washington, with art patrons Anne Gould Hauberg and John Hauberg. The school's summer program has become an international magnet for faculty and students working in glass.

Chihuly, assisted by a team of expert glassblowers, is perhaps the most prolific artist in the world. He has created many styles, or series, of objects and large-scale architectural installations over the years, but his Venetians have been prominent in his oeuvre for a decade. Initially, the "Venetian" series was a collaboration between Chihuly and Italian glass master Lino Tagliapietra. Chihuly sketched designs based on Venetian art deco glass from the 1920s, and Tagliapietra blew them. Chihuly recalls that "we had a great time putting these together—always going further, pushing beyond what we had done in each previous piece. Handles changed to knots, prunts became claws, colors went from subtle to bright, and forms from symmetrical to asymmetrical." Like the artist himself, his Venetians have become almost operatic in their flamboyance.

1. **Gilded Rose Venetian with Chartreuse Green Coil**
1990
60.96 x 40.64 x 38.10
Blown and sculpted glass
Claire Garoutte photograph
Lent by Dale Chihuly

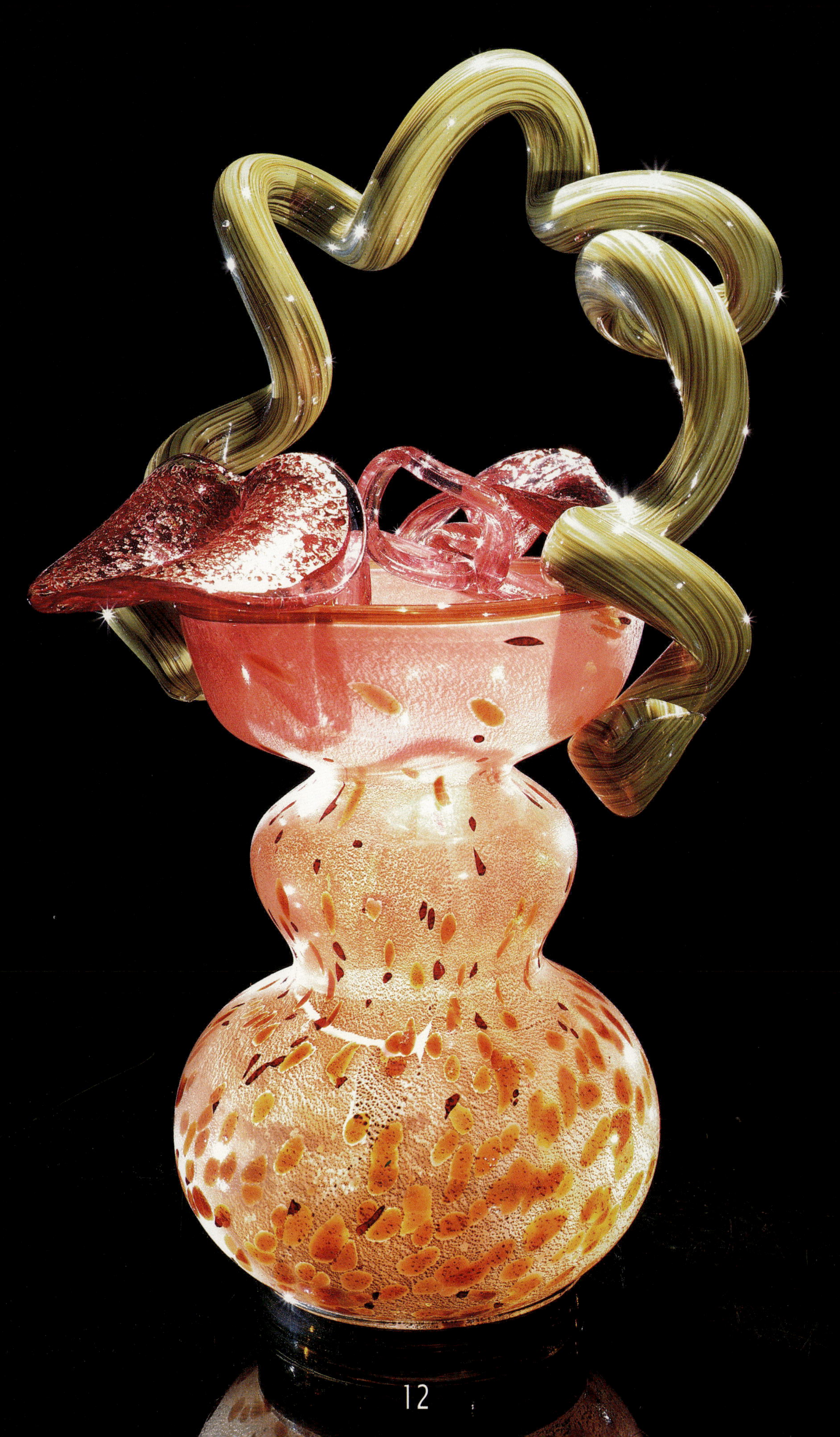

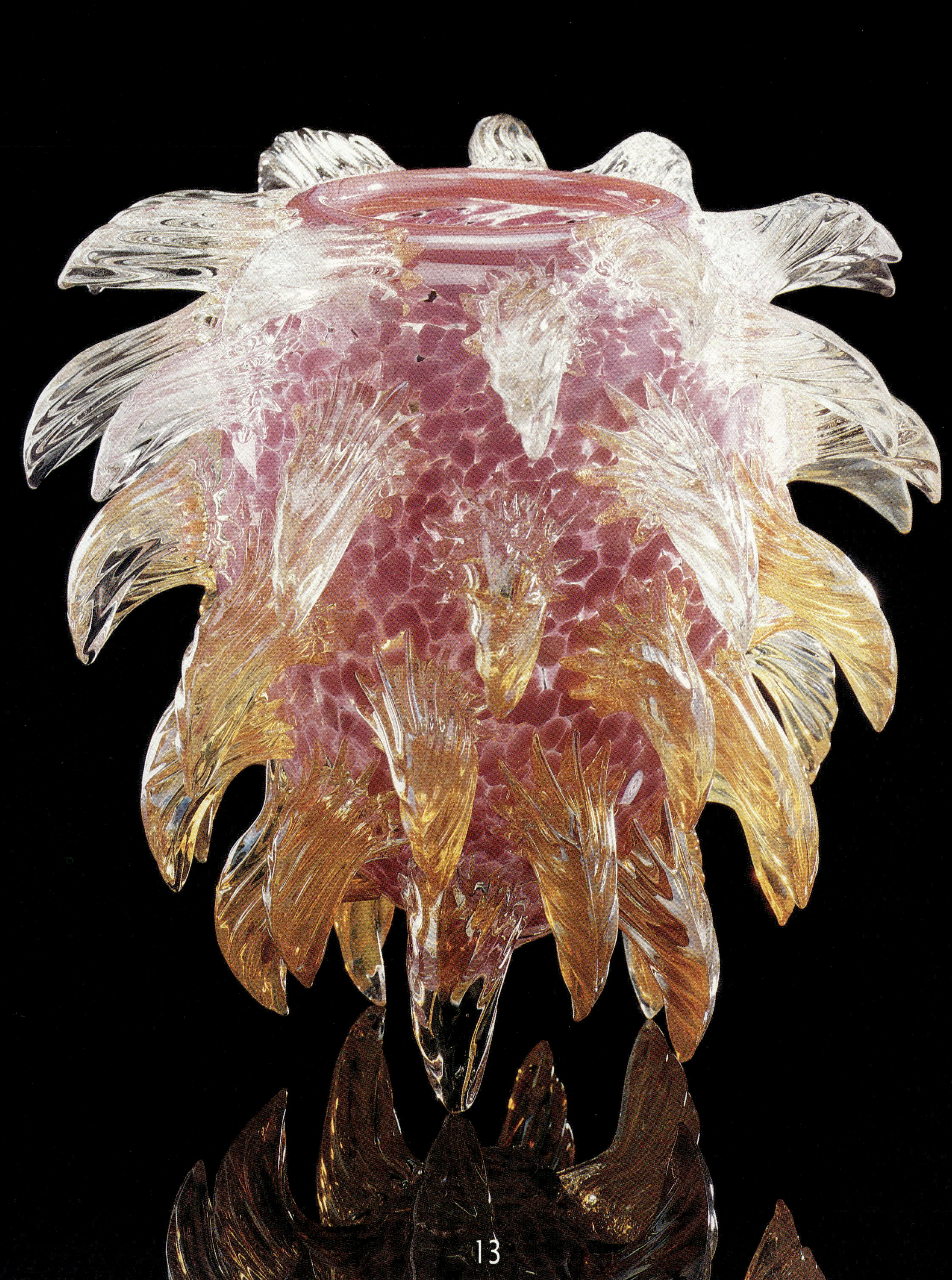

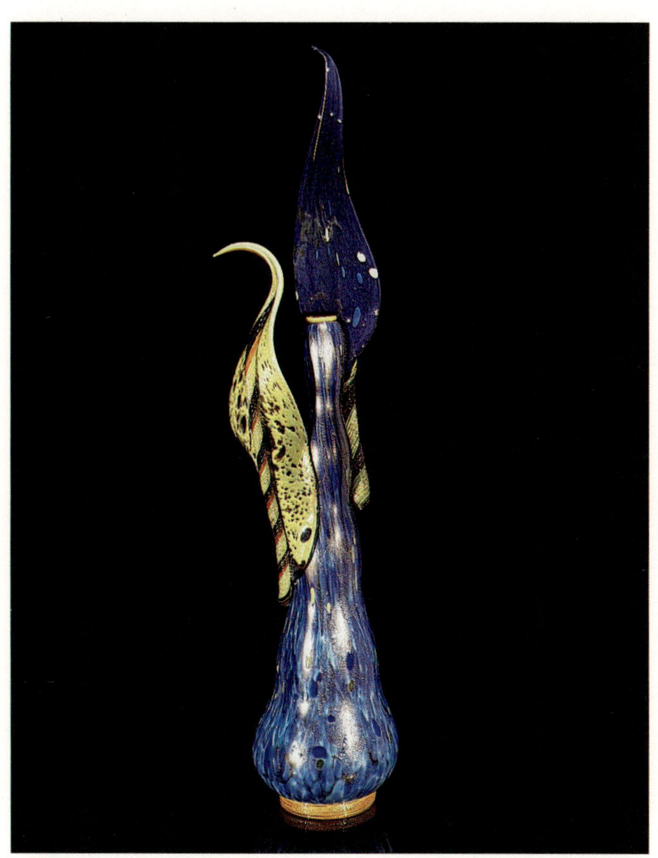

3. **Gold over Prussian Blue Venetian**
1990
111.76 x 35.56 x 33.02
Blown and sculpted glass
Claire Garoutte photograph
Lent by Dale Chihuly

4. **Cadmium Yellow Venetian with Umber Flowers**
1991
73.66 x 43.18 x 40.64
Blown and sculpted glass
Claire Garoutte photograph
Lent by Dale Chihuly

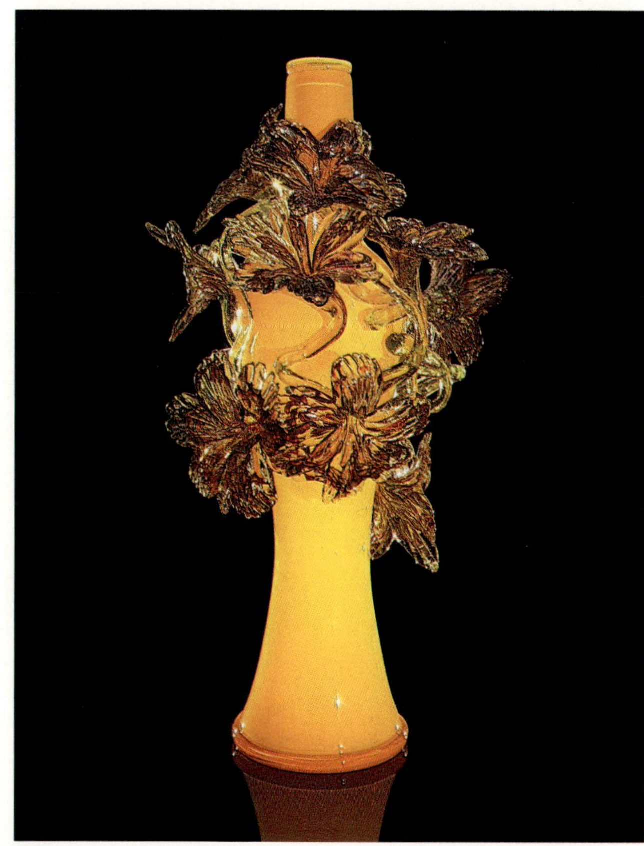

2. **Pink Venetian**
1990
38.10 x 43.18 x 40.64
Blown and sculpted glass
Roger Schreiber photograph
Lent by Dale Chihuly

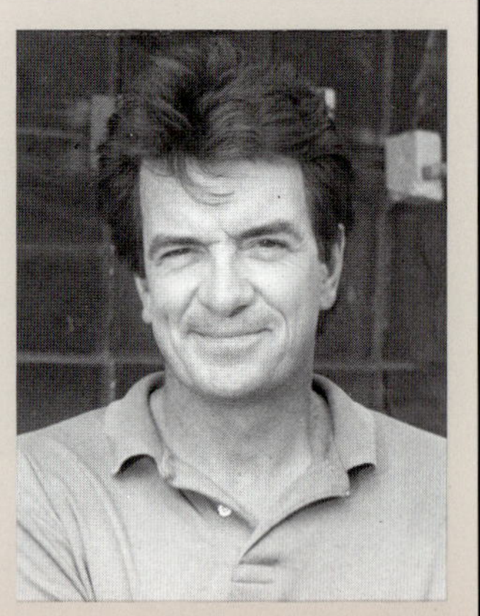

T. J. Sokol photograph, 1993

DAN DAILEY

Dan Dailey has been exhibiting his art in glass since 1968, when he built the Philadelphia College of Art's first glass studio while an undergraduate there. In 1972 he earned a master of fine arts degree from Rhode Island School of Design where he was the first graduate student in glass. After college, he worked for one year as a designer for the Venini factory while on a Fulbright fellowship to Venice. In 1974 he was asked to begin the glass program at Massachusetts College of Art, where he continues to teach.

Though a prolific artist exhibiting throughout the United States, and in recent years in Zurich, Paris, and Tokyo, since 1976 he has also designed glassware and makes limited-edition *pâte de verre* sculpture for Cristallerie Daum in France. In the United States he has designed for Fenton Art Glass Company, Steuben Glass, and the Herman Miller Company. Dailey is unique in his use of abstract figurative form and decoration, often employing human or social comment whether his glass sculptures are made from assembled sheet glass, blown forms with applied glass decoration, or sandblasted blown and enameled vessels.

"Almost everything I've made is subjective; it could be about a person, an animal, a feeling, an attitude, an emotion, a character. It might be an interpretation of an image or the depiction of an imagined being or it could be an illustration of a situation. I'm trying to communicate. I'm trying to evoke a response. I'm trying to speak to a viewer, but usually without words."

Dailey describes the heads shown here as "abstract in almost 'cubist' style, but since liquid glass imposes a fluidity, there is none of the harshness of the geometry often found in that style." His approach to abstracting form involves "reducing a form to its simplest elements, resulting in stylization. All from fairly obvious roots, but combined with the experience of my work of the past twenty years, these abstract heads have moved my vessels from a format for drawing to a dimensional interpretation of the drawing."

5. **Puff**
1992
52.07 x 38.10
Blown and sculpted glass
Lent by Dan Dailey

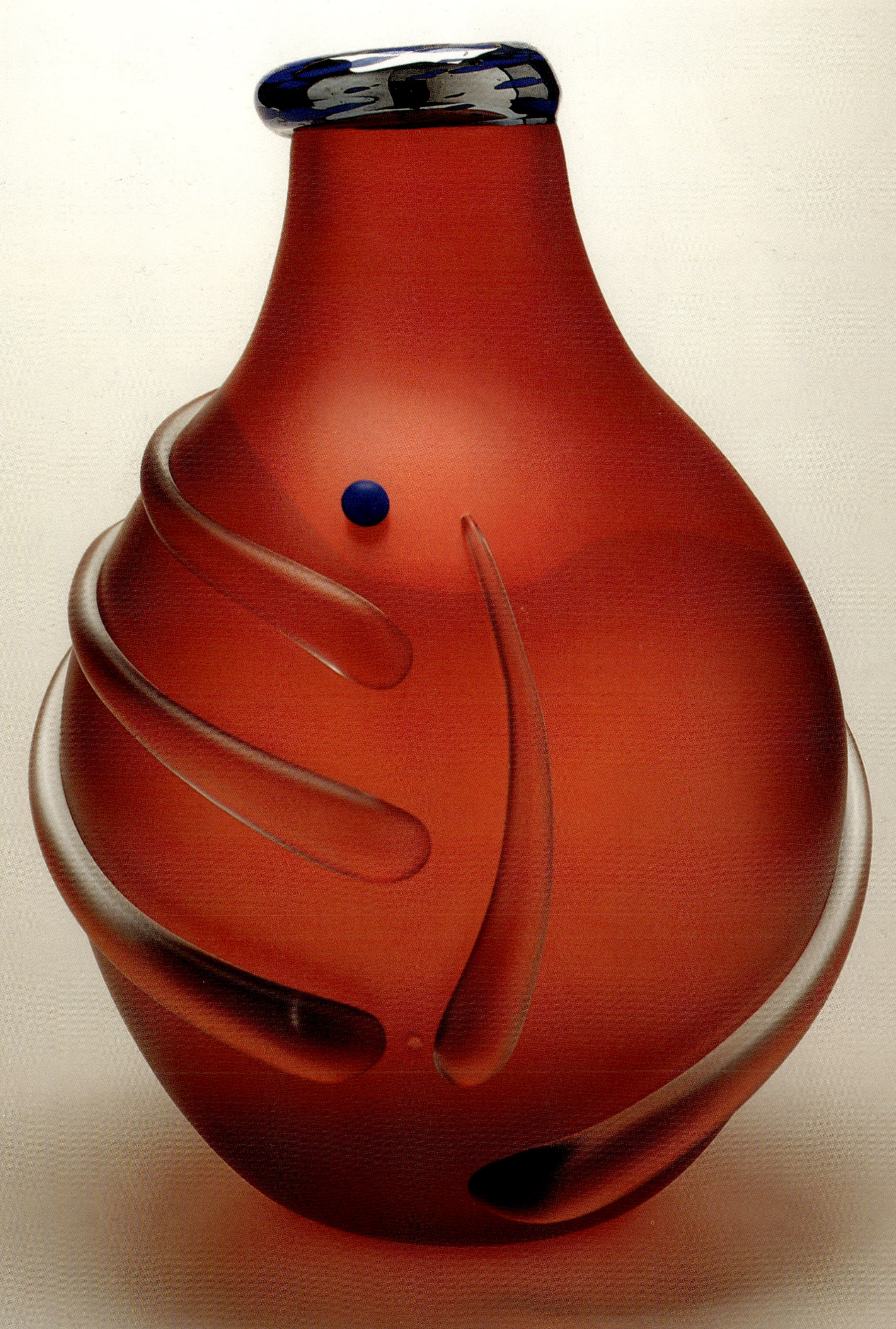

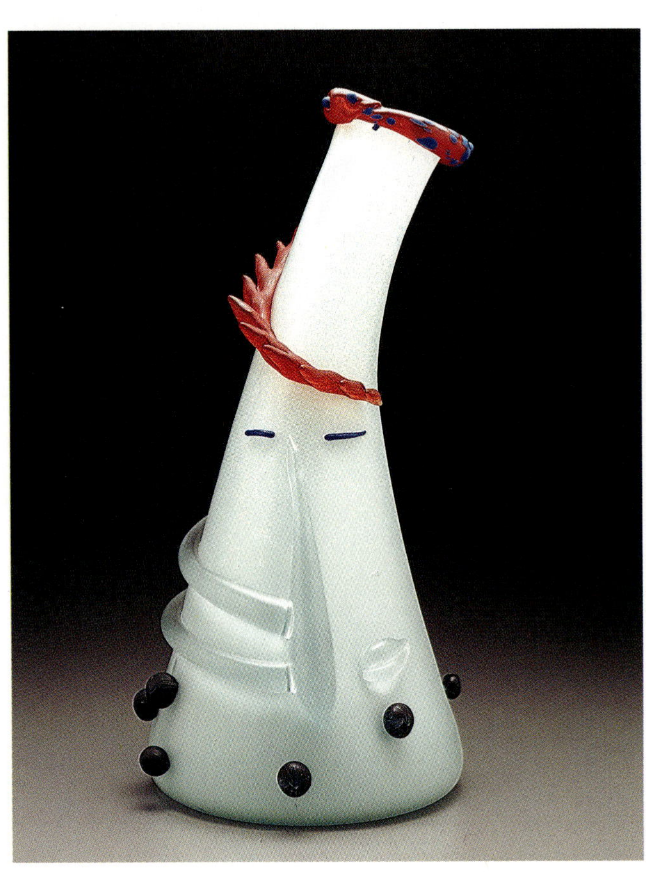

6. **Haute**
1991
63.50 x 27.94
Blown and sculpted glass
Lent by Dan Dailey

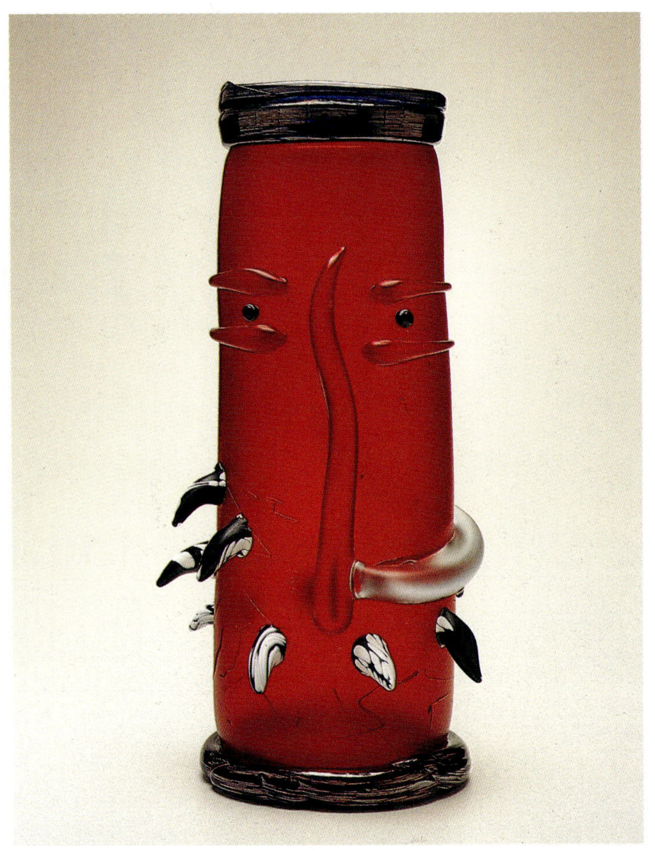

7. **Foreign**
1991
57.15 x 27.94
Blown and sculpted glass
Lent by Dan Dailey

8. **Serenity**
1994
58.42 x 33.02
Blown and sculpted glass
Lent by Dan Dailey

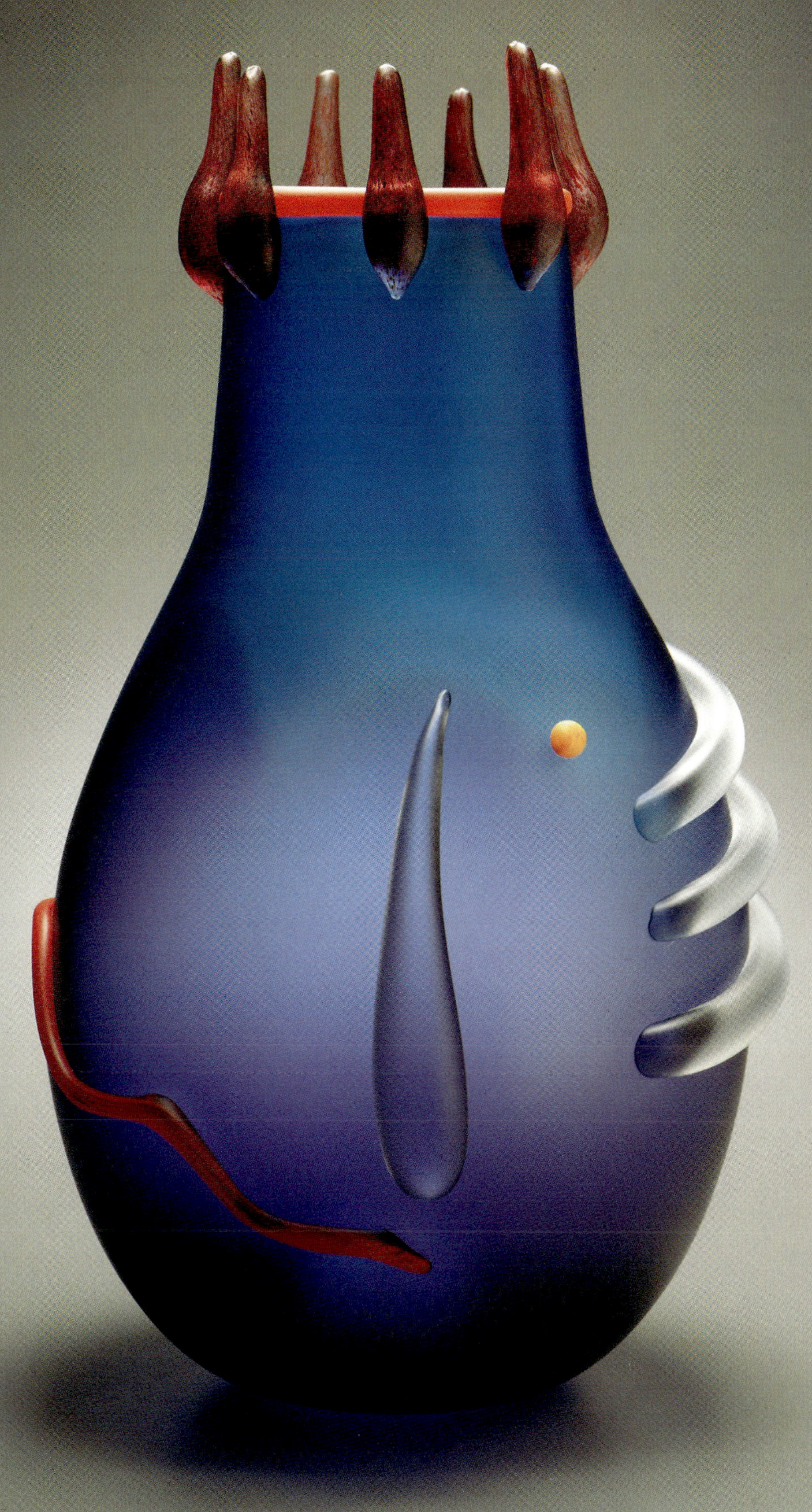

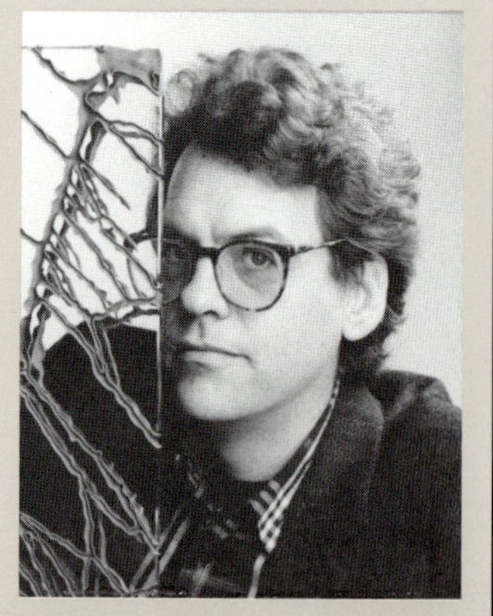

MICHAEL GLANCY

Rational but emotional, Michael Glancy's art is often described as "jewel-like." That is no accident. While earning a master of fine arts degree in Dale Chihuly's glass program at Rhode Island School of Design in the late 1970s, Glancy befriended jewelry students and often visited the jewelry department. He was attracted to the idea of combining glass with metal and found a way to do so through the process of electroforming.

Initially inspired by the artistry and technique of French glass artist Maurice Marinot, Glancy emulated him by using hydrofluoric acid to carve deep gridlike patterns into glass. On discovering the sandblaster at Pilchuck Glass School in 1977, Glancy mastered a variety of cutting techniques for carving into his thick-walled blown glass vessels. The areas to be left uncut are masked with a self-adhesive rubber stencil like those used in cutting names into gravestones.

Glancy's originality lies in both his style and his process. The process of electroforming electrically charges atoms of metal and causes them to "jacket" his sculpted glass vessels. "I particularly like copper because of the colors that can be achieved on the metals and with oxidation," he has said.

The development of his format of a vase resting on a platform, united by patterning, came accidentally. Making three-dimensional sketches on flat paper for the carving of his vase forms wasn't entirely satisfactory, so he began "drawing" on sheets of plate glass. It occurred to him that the glass sketches were themselves objects and were intimately related to the vases. The union of the two forms has given him seemingly limitless possibilities of creating dialogues between the two. "I am very pleased that this might take the rest of my life and even then I'll never be bored with it and never have finished."

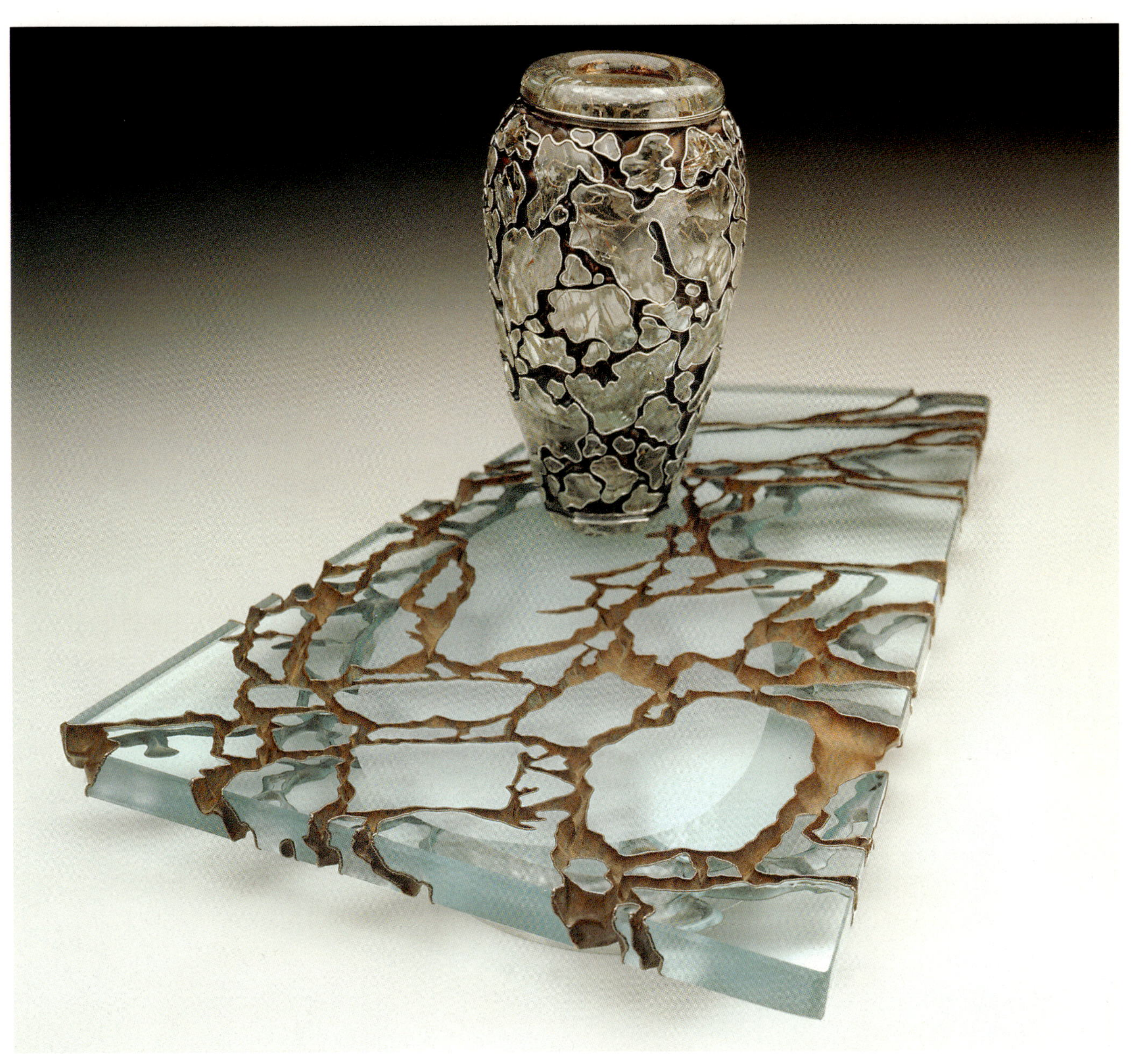

9. **Crystal Obscura**
Base 1986; Object 1998
15.24 x 20.32 x 38.1
Blown glass; industrial plate glass; silver; copper
Gene Dwiggins photograph
Lent by Daniel Greenberg and Susan Steinhauser

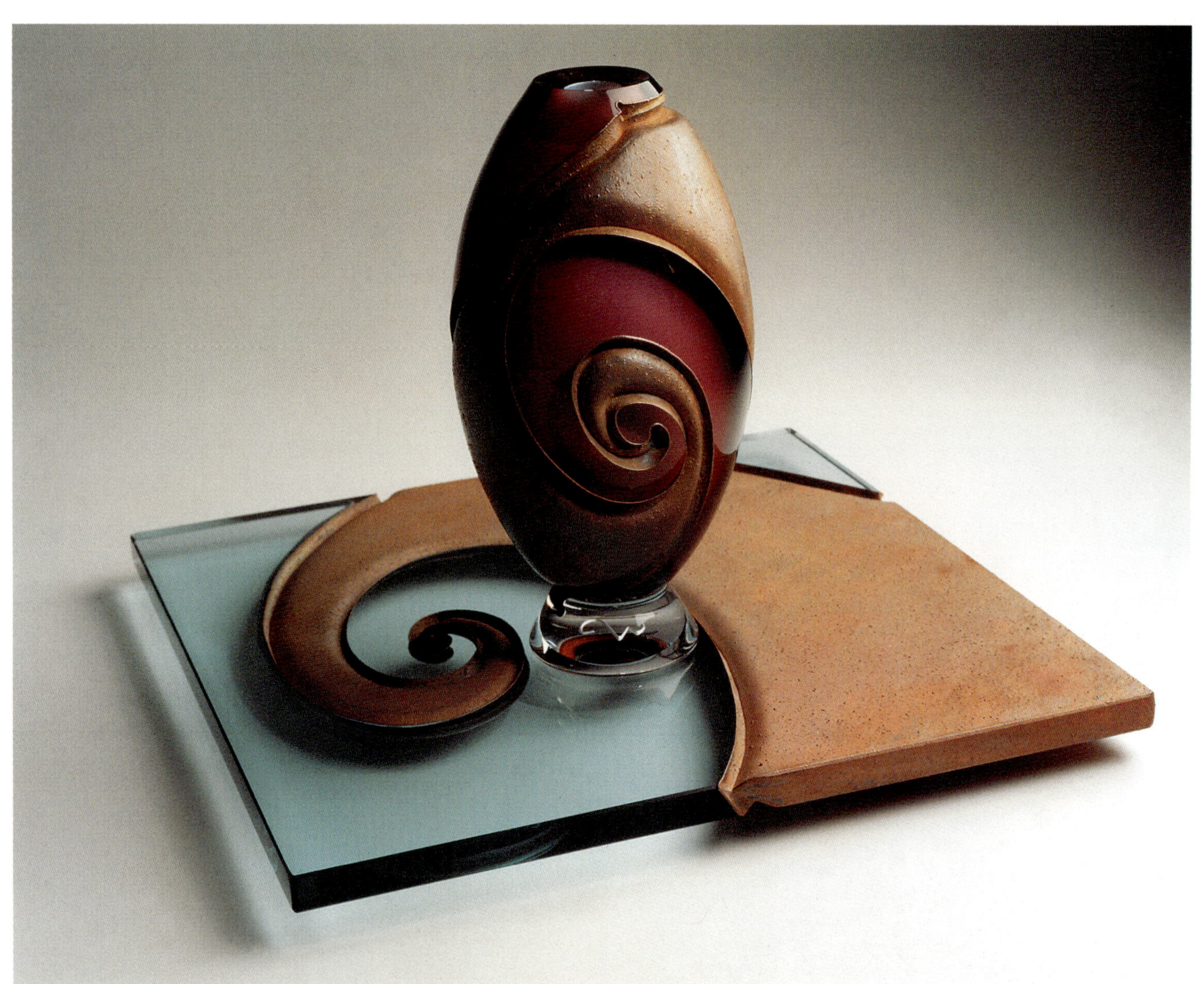

10. **The Still Point**
1991
35.56 x 45.72 x 45.72
Blown glass; industrial plate glass; copper
Lent by Michael Glancy, courtesy of Galerie von Bartha, Basel, Switzerland

11. **Tricolored Cohesian**
1994
21.59 x 19.05 x 19.05
Blown glass; copper; silver and gold
Lent by Daniel Greenberg and Susan Steinhauser

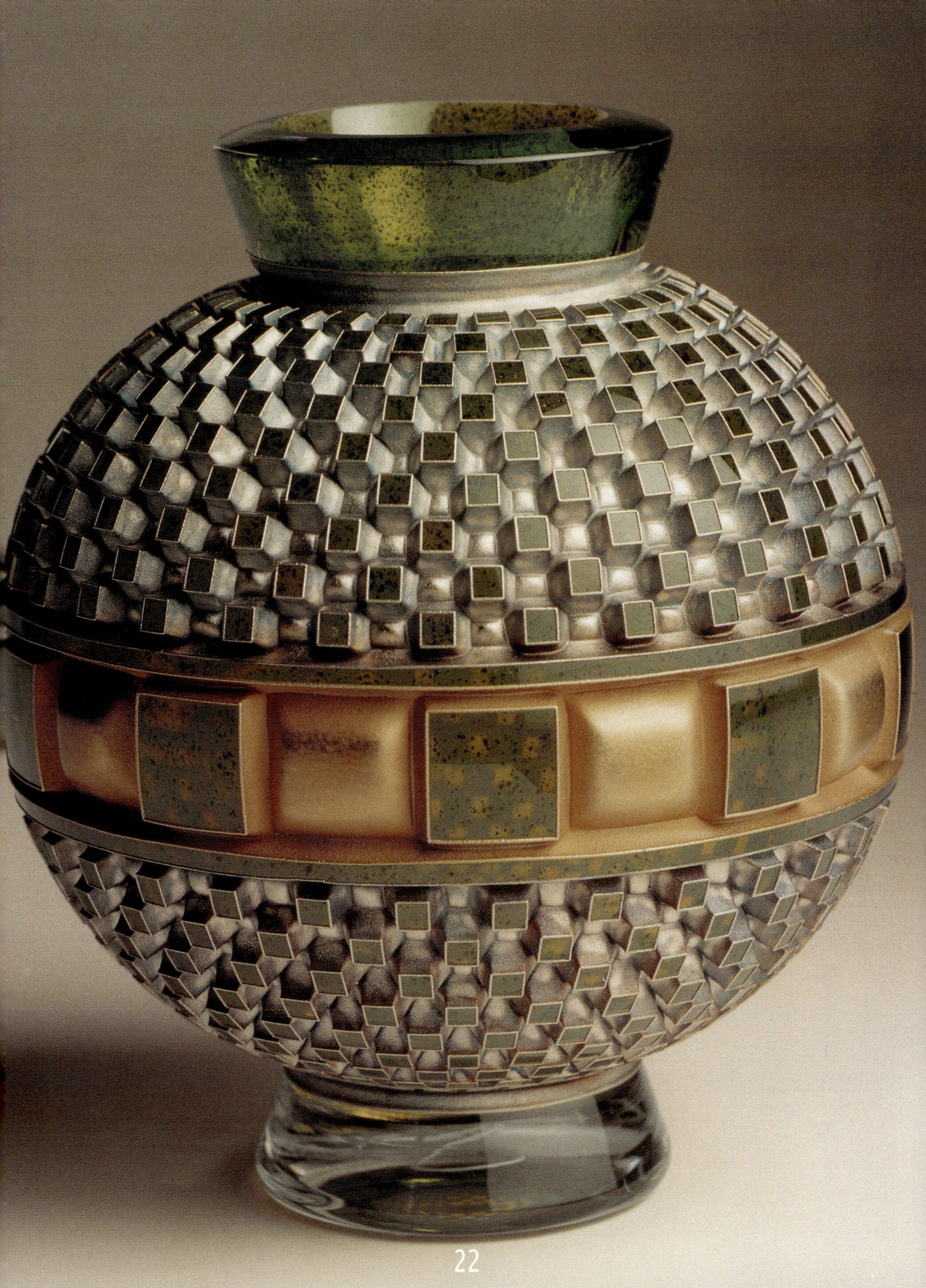

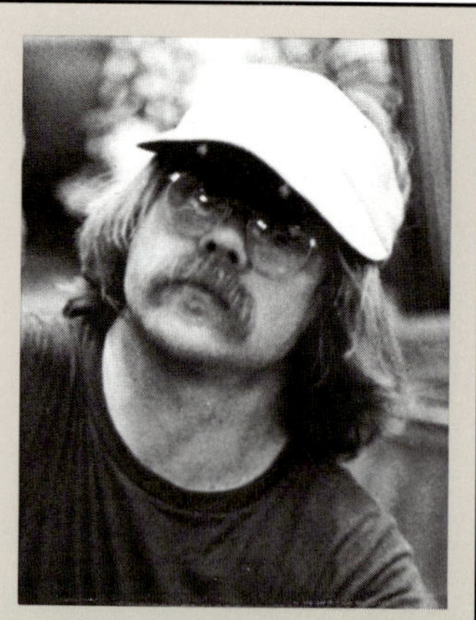
Vigiletti photograph

RICHARD MARQUIS

Richard Marquis is the American master of Venetian glassworking processes and often incorporates into his art both *zanfirico (latticinio* in England and America), to create filigree or lace patterning in glass, and *murrine,* in which glass rods are made and, cut in cross section, reveal patterns or pictures. Though incorporating such techniques, his art is distinctly American in form and often incorporates a wry sense of humor.

He learned to blow glass at the University of California at Berkeley (and later headed the glass program at the University of California at Los Angeles) but wanted to go to Italy to study Venetian techniques. Receiving a Fulbright fellowship in 1969, he prepared a speech in Italian to deliver to Venetian glass factory owners, proposing to work in exchange for instruction. He was given the opportunity to work for a year at the Venini factory.

Perhaps because he was a potter before learning to manipulate molten glass, Marquis has for years made teapots—not to hold and pour tea, but as decorative objects that serve as vehicles for his exuberant use of color and pattern. Here the teapots are incorporated in the stems of goblets and as "sample" boxes like a manufacturer might use to display a variety of wares.

The "sample box" idea for Marquis also refers to his own interest in collecting a wide variety of ordinary manufactured objects, often in their original store displays. Occasionally he incorporates cheap salt and pepper shakers from his vast collection into his sculptures. Because he eschews preciousness while employing meticulous techniques often identified with precious objects, Marquis often also casually applies paint to the surfaces of his pieces. He encourages viewers to look beyond the humor in his work to recognize elements of design and his use of color and form.

12. **Coffeepot Sample Box**
1993-94
48.83 x 30.48 x 9.84
Blown glass; mixed media
Rob Vinnedge photograph
Lent by Kate Elliott, Elliot Brown Gallery, Seattle, Washington

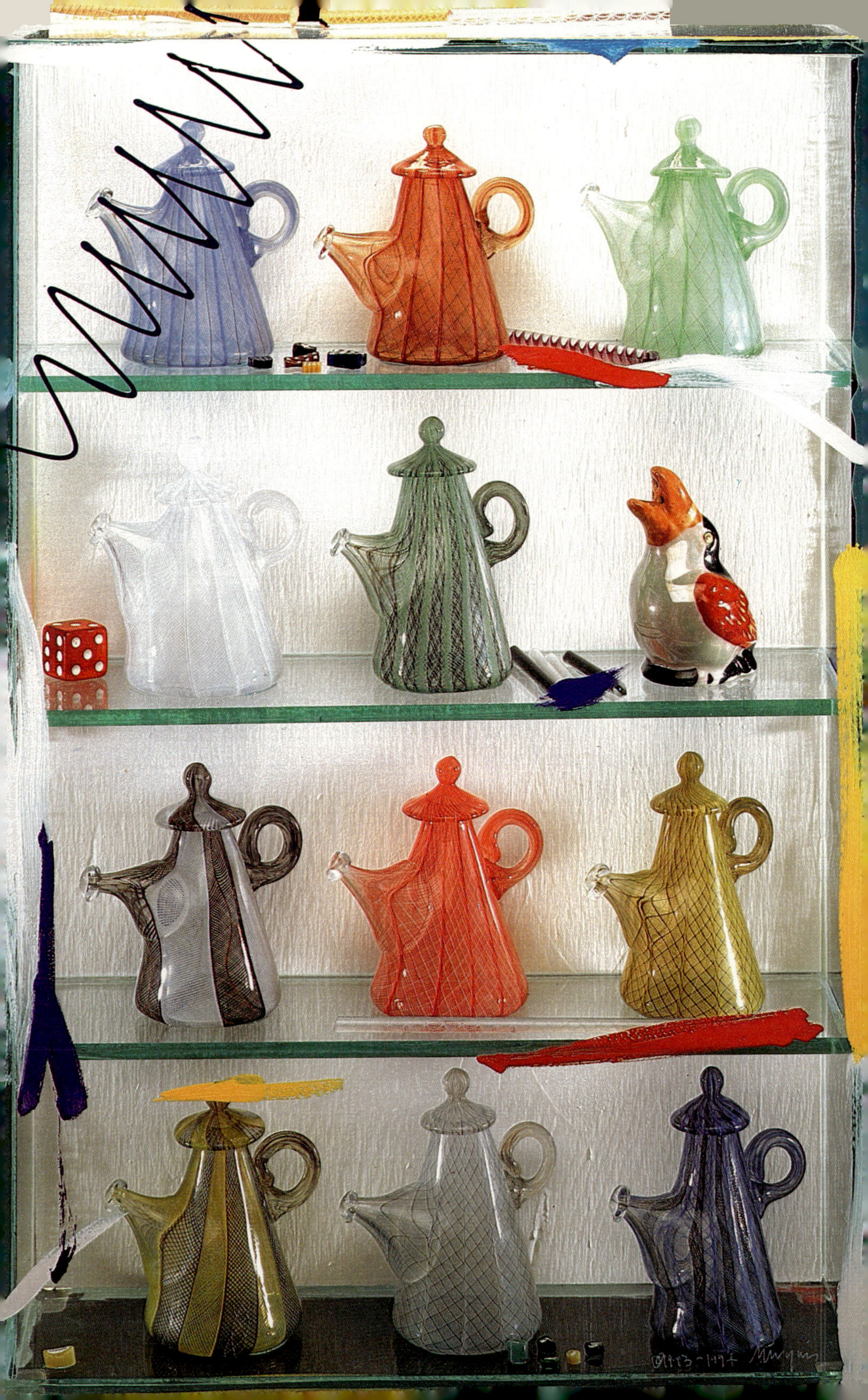

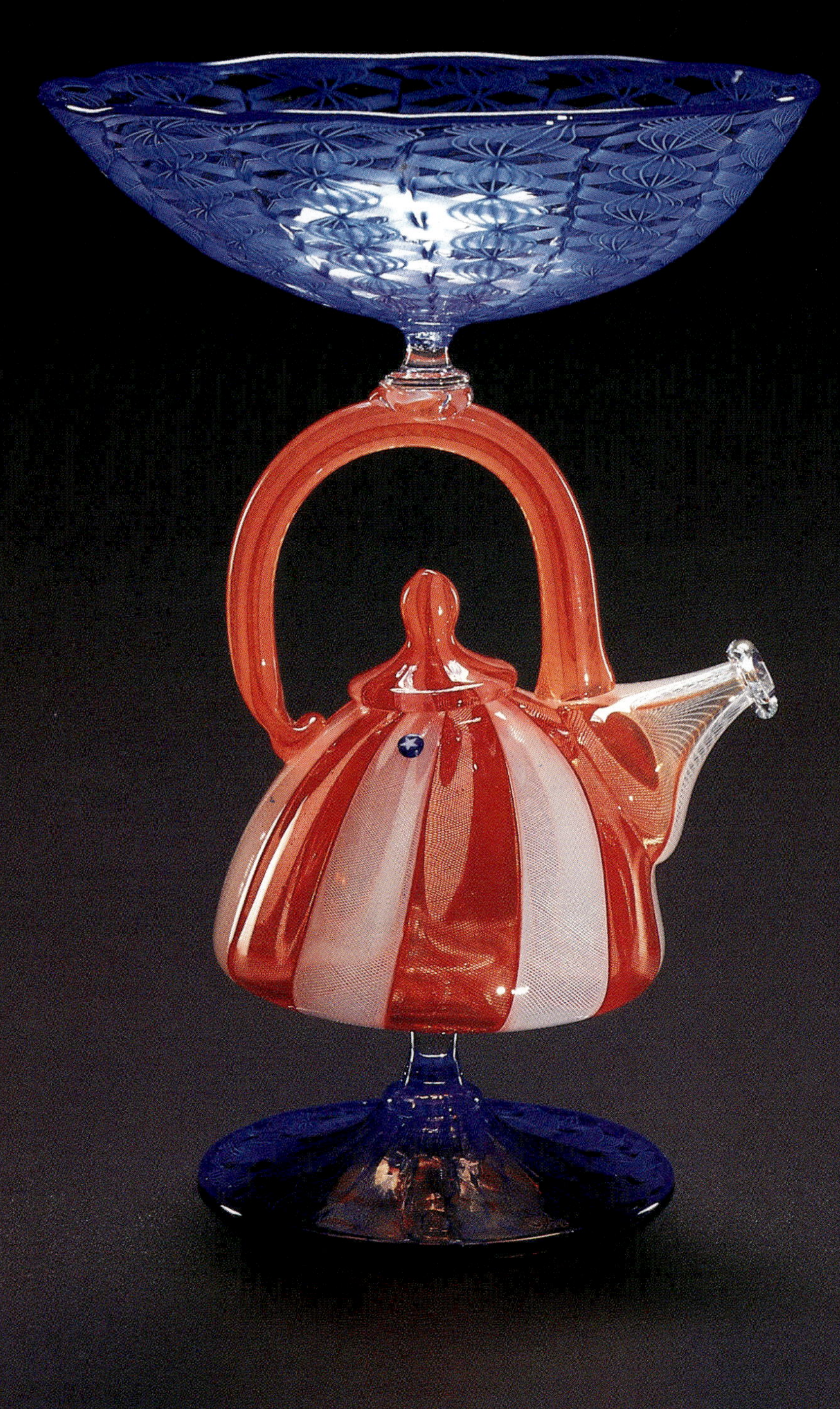

14. **Teapot Goblet #219**
1990
26.67 x 10.16 x 8.25
Blown glass
Rob Vinnedge photograph
Lent by Arthur Liu

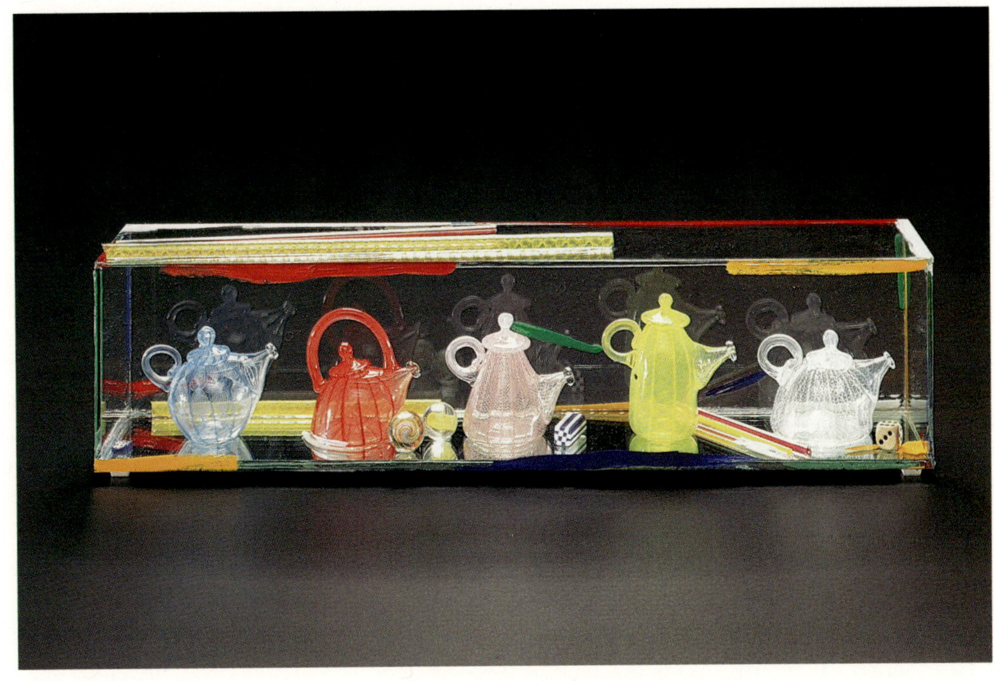

16. **Teapot Box #3**
1993
14.60 x 52.07 x 10.16
Blown glass; mixed media
Rob Vinnedge photograph
Lent by Arthur Liu

13. **Teapot Goblet**
1990
27.94 x 10.16 x 8.89
Blown glass
Rob Vinnedge photograph
Lent by Kate Elliott, Elliot Brown Gallery,
Seattle, Washington

15. **Teapot Goblet 94-12**
1994
20 x 14.28
Blown glass
Rob Vinnedge photograph
Lent by Arthur Liu

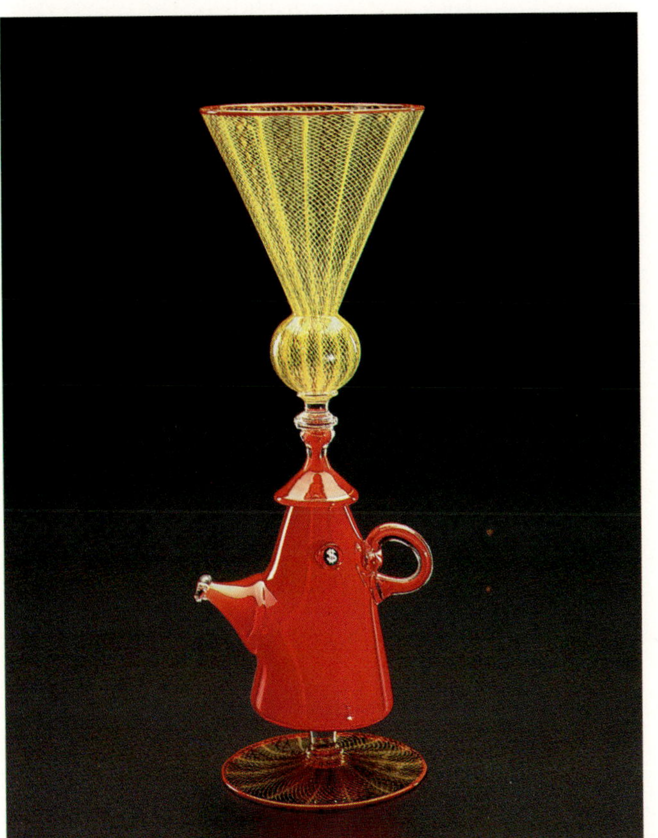

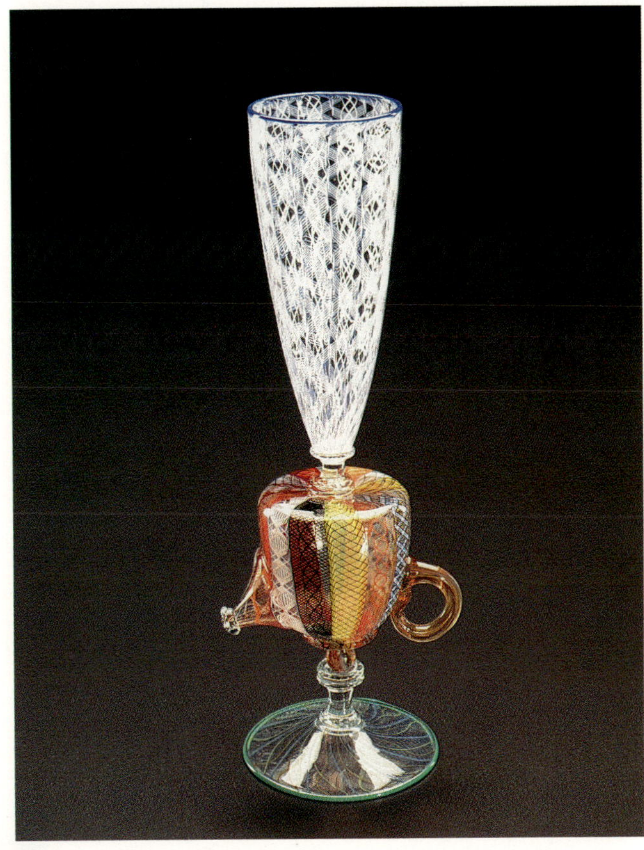

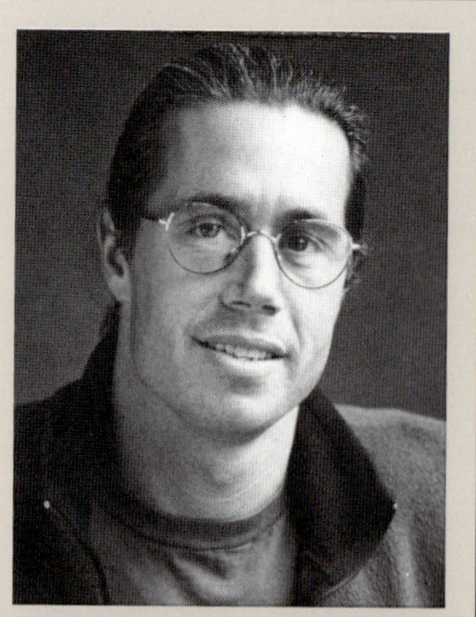
Rob Vinnedge photograph

WILLIAM MORRIS

In his unique glass sculpture, William Morris weds his fascination with the archeological past and his avocation as a hunter with bow and arrow. A prolific and popular artist, he has progressively found and used inspiration from antiquity in his "Standing Stones" and "Artifacts" series. His blown forms have been richly decorated with scenes of the hunt that might have been drawn onto cave walls, and he has combined glass skulls and bones, antlers, teeth, and primitive tools into exquisite assemblages—some of them room-size installations.

Along with his recent "Hanging Artifacts," the "Canopic Jars" extend his interest in form, surface, and the mystery of the past. The series, based on the ancient Egyptian lidded vases that were made to hold embalmed entrails in the tombs of the pharaohs, resulted from a more ambitious opportunity for a commissioned work of art. In 1992, collector George Stroemple approached Morris about making an Egyptian-style tomb from glass, and the artist suggested working first on a small aspect of the project. Those first jars portrayed the four children of the Egyptian god Horus—a falcon, baboon, man, and jackal—all sculpted in glass.

While hunting the following fall, Morris began to contemplate the spiritual aspects of animals' life and death and continued the "Canopic Jar" series with animals he had seen in nature. Later jars were based on more exotic species. Morris developed his specialized process of sculpting hot glass to make the animal heads for the jars' lids after studying related techniques in Venice in 1988. The visual quality possible with glass is important to the artist, who also prizes his material for its permanence, timelessness and fragility.

17. **Canopic Jar: Buck**
1992
104.14 x 30.48
Blown and sculpted glass
Rob Vinnedge photograph
Lent by Gary Werths

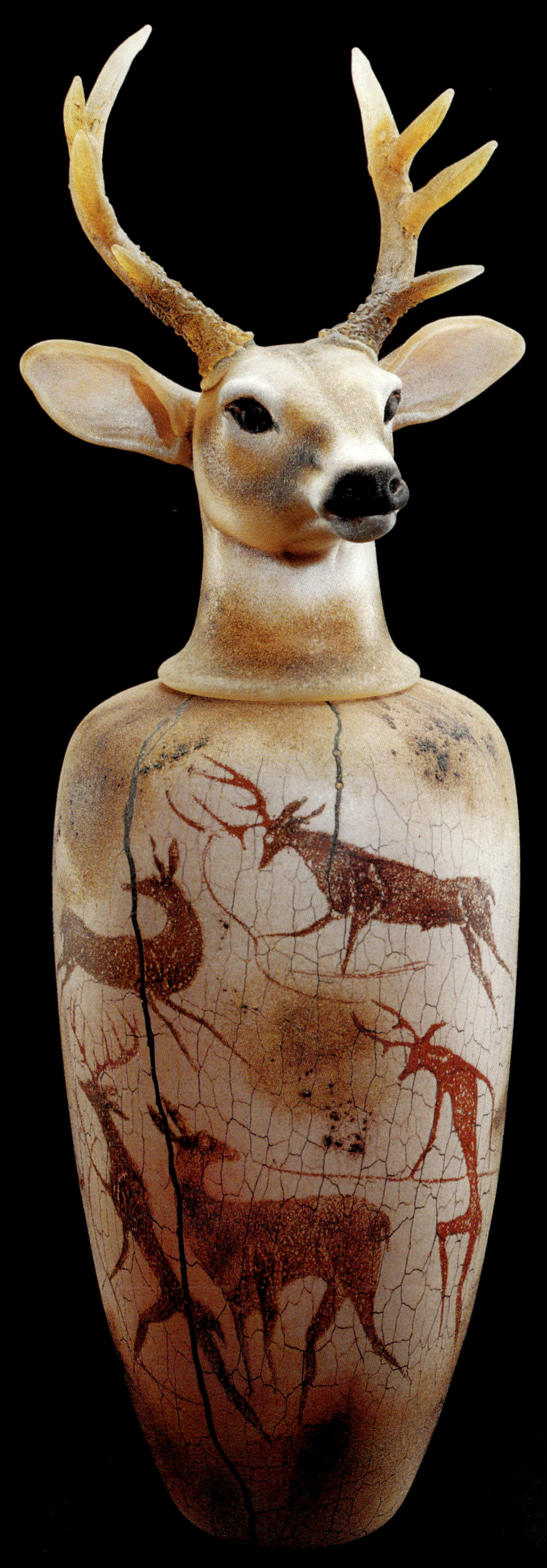

18. **Canopic Jar: Dahl Sheep**
1994
91.44 x 50.80 x 38.10
Blown and sculpted glass
Rob Vinnedge photograph
Lent by the George R. Stroemple Collection, Portland, Oregon

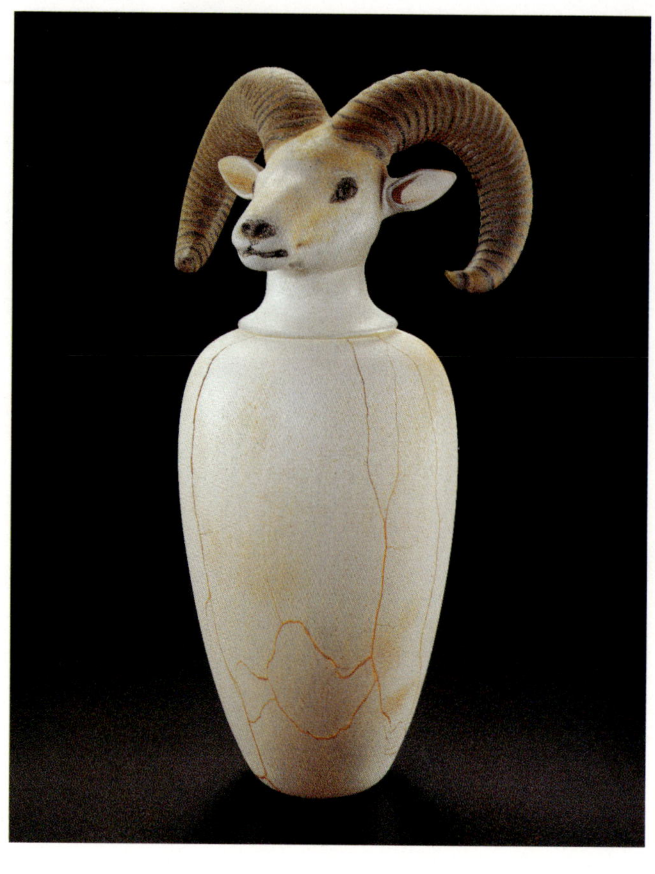

19. **Canopic Jar: Gazelle**
1995
132.08 x 30.48
Blown and sculpted glass
Rob Vinnedge photograph
Lent by the George R. Stroemple Collection, Portland, Oregon

20. **Canopic Jar: Hawk**
1995
68.58 x 25.4
Blown and sculpted glass
Rob Vinnedge photograph
Lent by William Morris

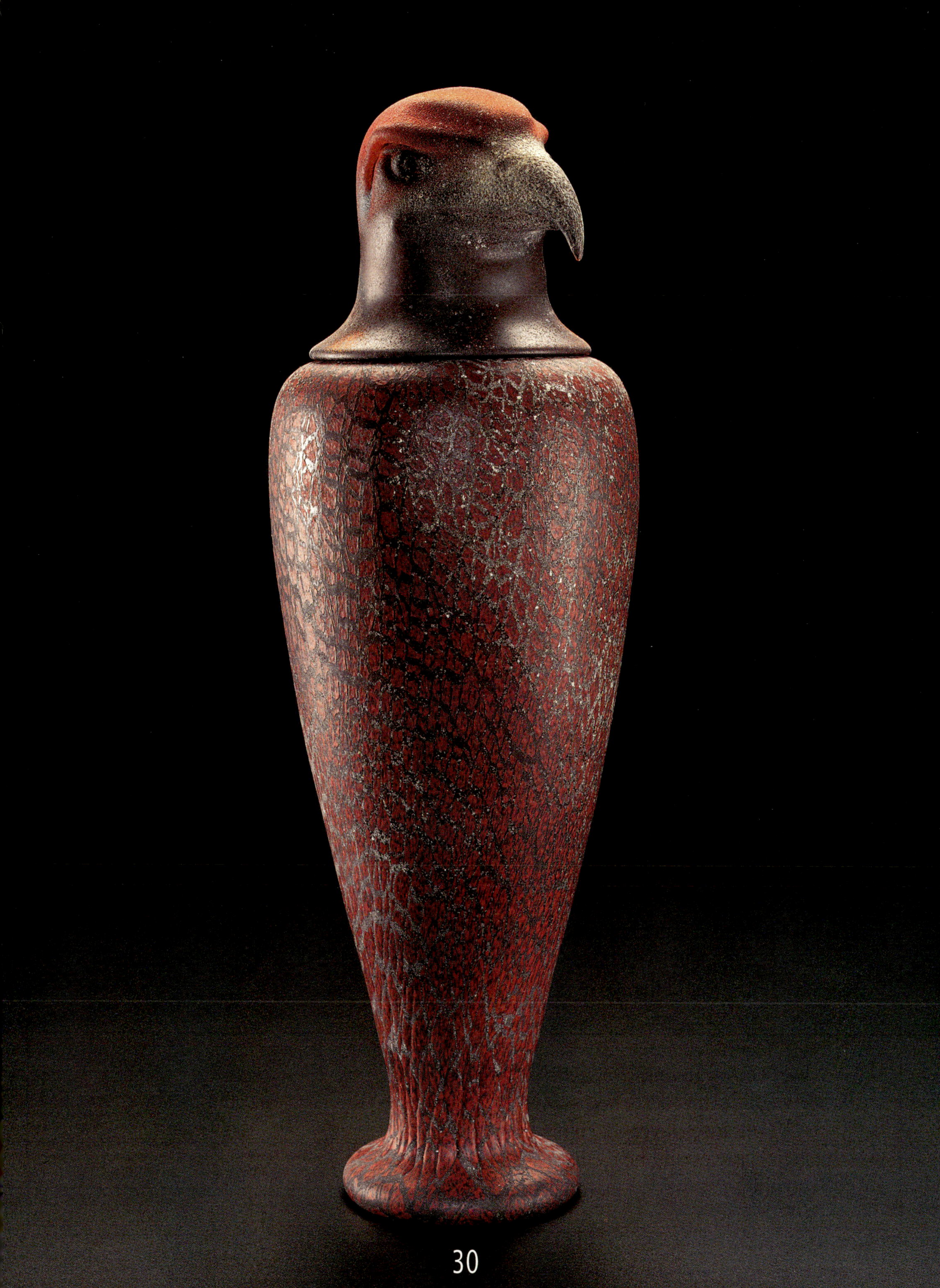

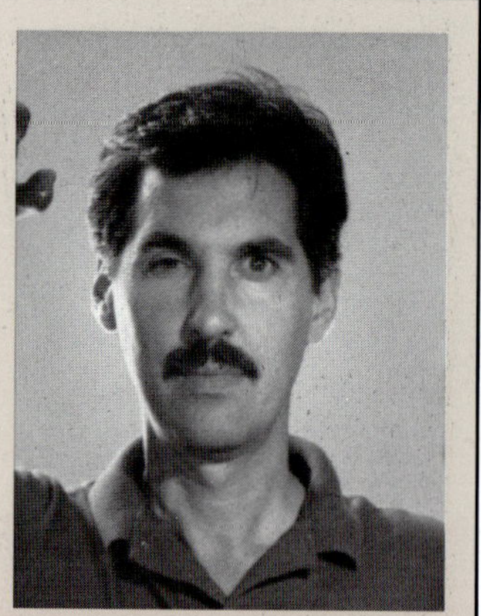

Paul J. Rocheleau photograph

THOMAS PATTI

The precision of Thomas Patti's nearly solid glass vessels may be traced to his education as an industrial designer and his investigation of art and its relationship to science and technology. Following his graduation in 1969 with a master of fine arts degree from Pratt Institute, he worked in architectural design and as a consultant.

He first exhibited his glass art in 1978. Both the Museum of Modern Art and the Metropolitan Museum of Art in New York City immediately acquired pieces for their permanent collections. A year later his work received international visibility when it was chosen in the worldwide competition sponsored by The Corning Museum of Glass (Corning, New York) for the exhibition titled *New Glass* and was featured on the cover of the exhibition catalogue. More than two dozen museums around the world now own his art.

Developing his own unique process of working glass, which he has described as "blown/laminated," Patti fuses layers of commercial and industrial glasses and heats the resulting form to the point that he can manipulate the shape into a seemingly solid mass. His work is minimal and subtle in its visual effects. He uses color sparingly, to stratify light and define the form.

"The process of discovery inspires my work," the artist says, "creating a visual language of logic for the exploration of science and art. I try to create a dialogue between perception and recognition through my work. Glass reveals for me the physical science of our universe—the origins of creation on the molecular scale. I discard art's historical reference to pursue the pure, elemental, and spiritual. They are conceptual details, undisturbed and silent."

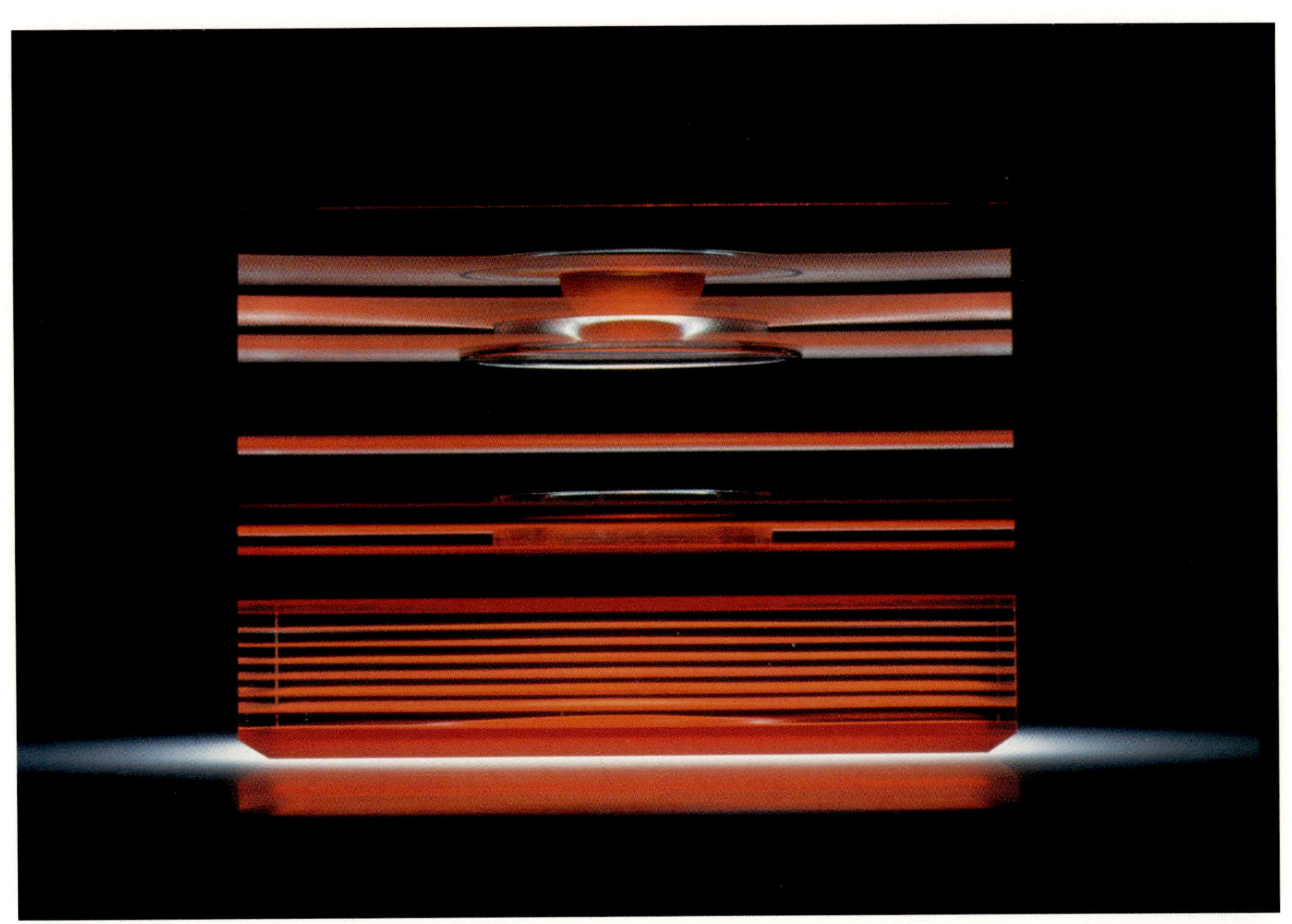

21. **Red Lumina with Compound Disk**
1991
10.31 x 14.12 x 9.98
Fused, hand-shaped, ground and polished glass
Lent by the Patti Collection, Plainfield, Massachusetts

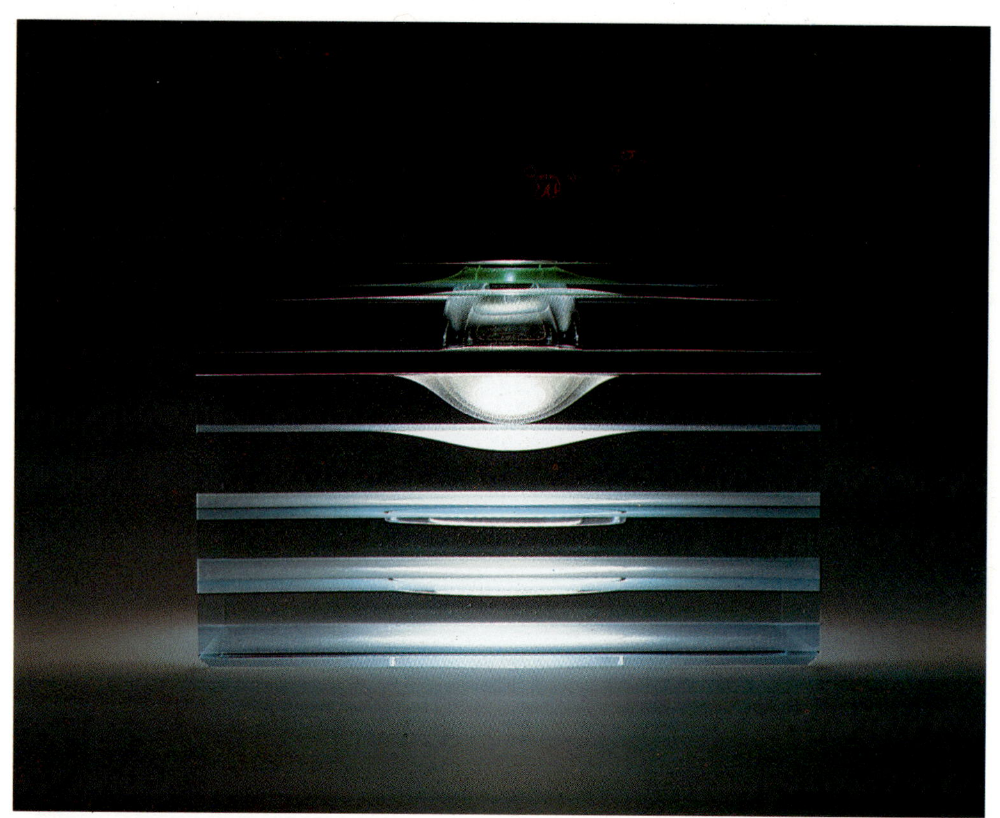

22. **Black Echo with Green**
1992
10.16 x 15.87 x 11.43
Fused, hand-shaped, ground and polished glass
Lent by the Patti Collection, Plainfield, Massachusetts

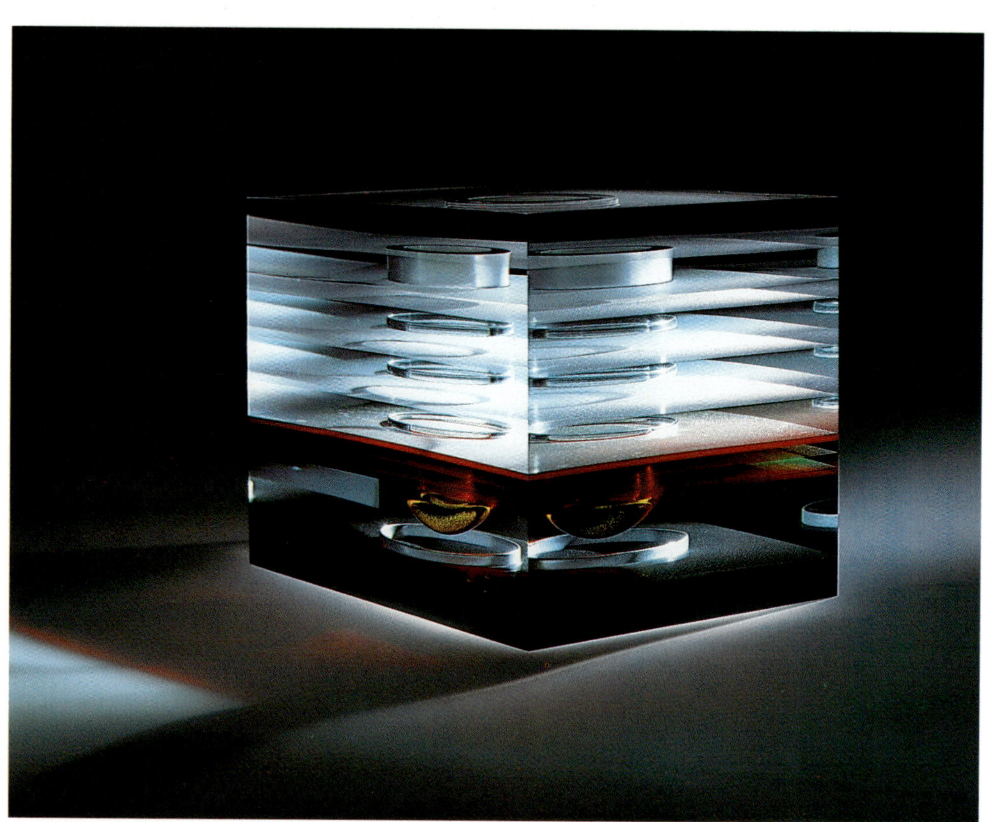

23. **Green Lumina Echo with Red**
1993
12.36 x 14.27 x 11.09
Fused, hand-shaped, ground and polished glass
Lent by the Patti Collection, Plainfield, Massachusetts

24. **Starphire Lumina with Blue, Green, Red and Mirrorized Disk**
1994
10.31 x 15.06 x 11.32
Fused, hand-shaped, ground and polished glass
Lent by the Patti Collection, Plainfield, Massachusetts

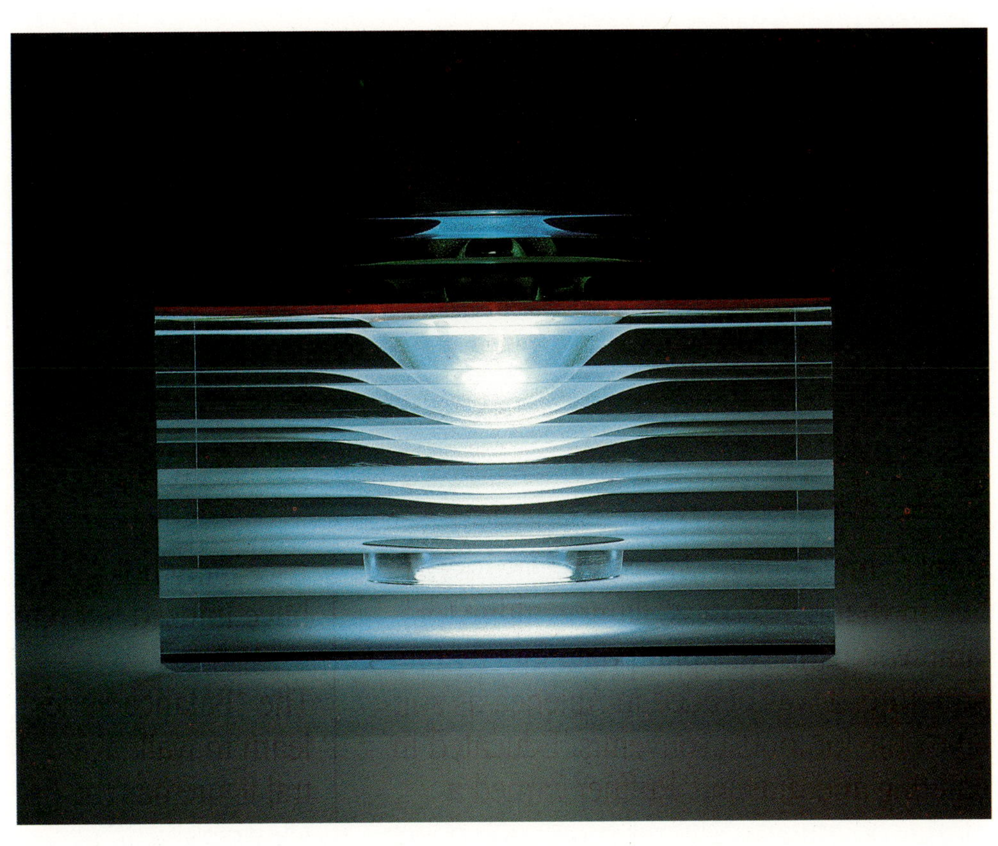

25. **Spectral Starphire Clear with Mirrorized Disk, Orange and Black**
1994-95
11.02 x 14.90 x 10.79
Fused, hand-shaped, ground and polished glass
Lent by the Patti Collection, Plainfield, Massachusetts

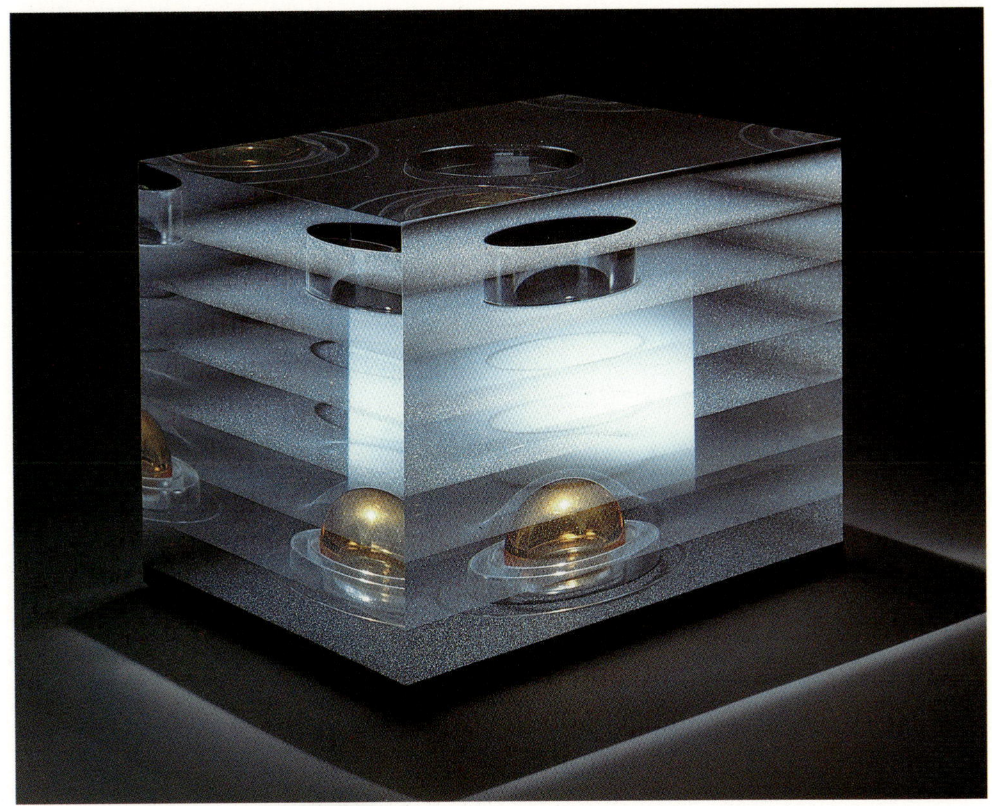

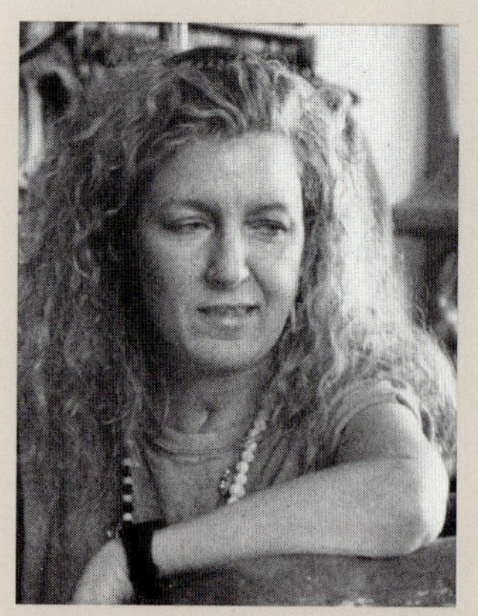

Julie Haack photograph

GINNY RUFFNER

Until Ginny Ruffner demonstrated through her art that her process, flameworking (or lampworking), was appropriate for creating sculpture, it was derided in America as suitable only for tourist souvenirs. Educated in painting and drawing, Ruffner earned a master of fine arts summa cum laude degree from the University of Georgia in 1975. Painting continues to be important in her art, whether on canvas or the glass sculptures that have brought her recognition in public and private collections across the United States.

In 1991, Ruffner was severely injured in an automobile collision. Regaining consciousness after five weeks in a coma, through regular and rigorous physical therapy she has combated serious compromise to her left side and has resumed work as an artist and workshop teacher.

Working with assistants to physically fabricate each sculpture, Ruffner uses softened laboratory glass tubes to "draw" in space. Then, using pencil, paint, and dye—"whatever will work"—the imagery on the glass surface is developed. Art historical references, mythology, and contemporary life all have infused her painted sculpture.

The "Balance Series" concerns her efforts to learn to walk again. In each piece, the central figure has the head of a cat, a fox or a Martian ("things we assume to be 'intelligent' "), is attired in a black and white ("because we have a tendency to view things in a black and white, diametrically opposed, polar opposites manner") tee shirt and pants and suggests juggling or acrobatics.

"The figure is usually balancing things in its hands and is balancing him/herself on an appropriate object or a beam made of an object, or supported by evocative objects," the artist says. "I chose an alter ego of a completely different species or a space alien to indicate how strange and foreign it feels not to be a biped. The series is evolving from being solely about learning to walk to a comment on the daily balancing act we all do, especially regarding decisions and choices."

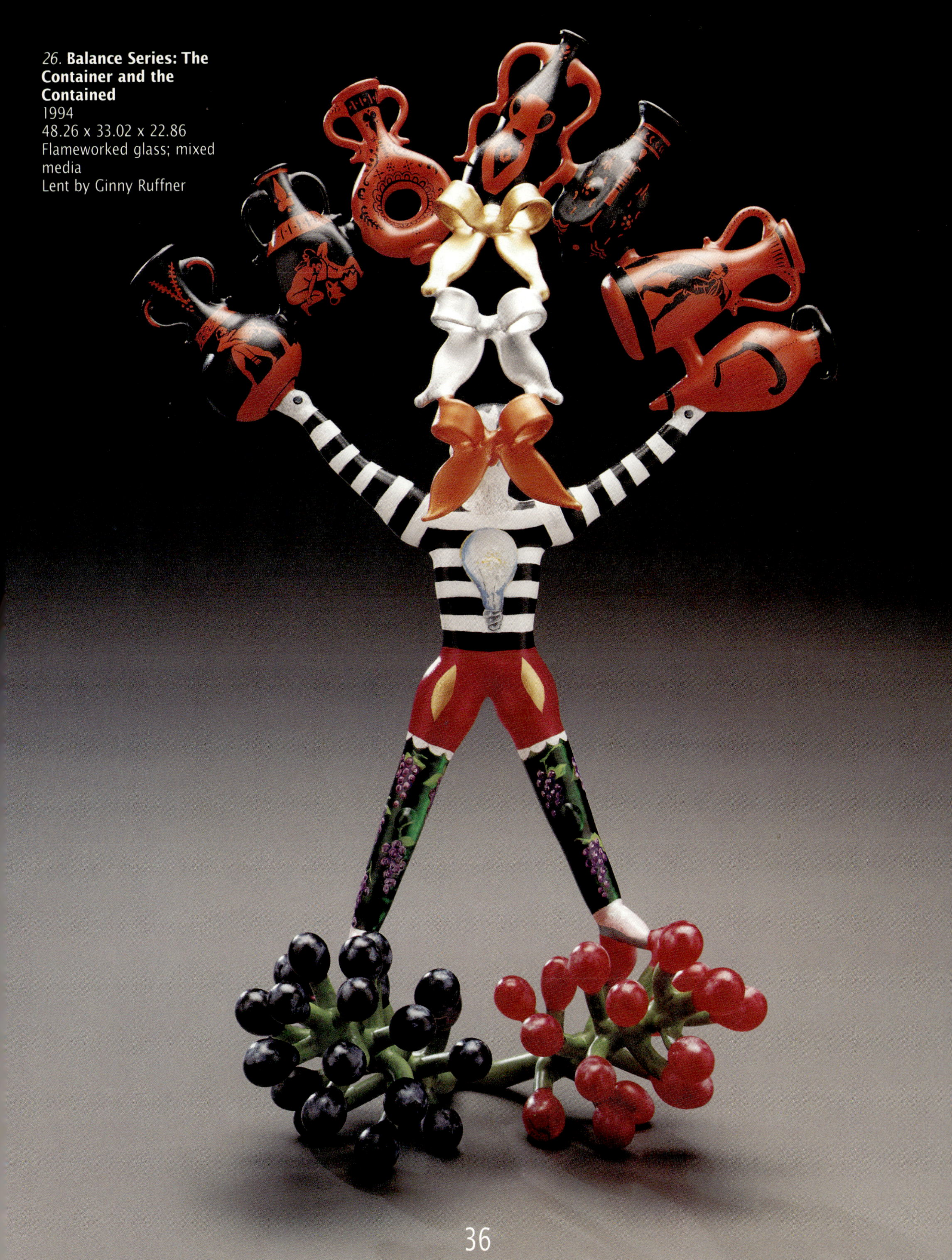

26. **Balance Series: The Container and the Contained**
1994
48.26 x 33.02 x 22.86
Flameworked glass; mixed media
Lent by Ginny Ruffner

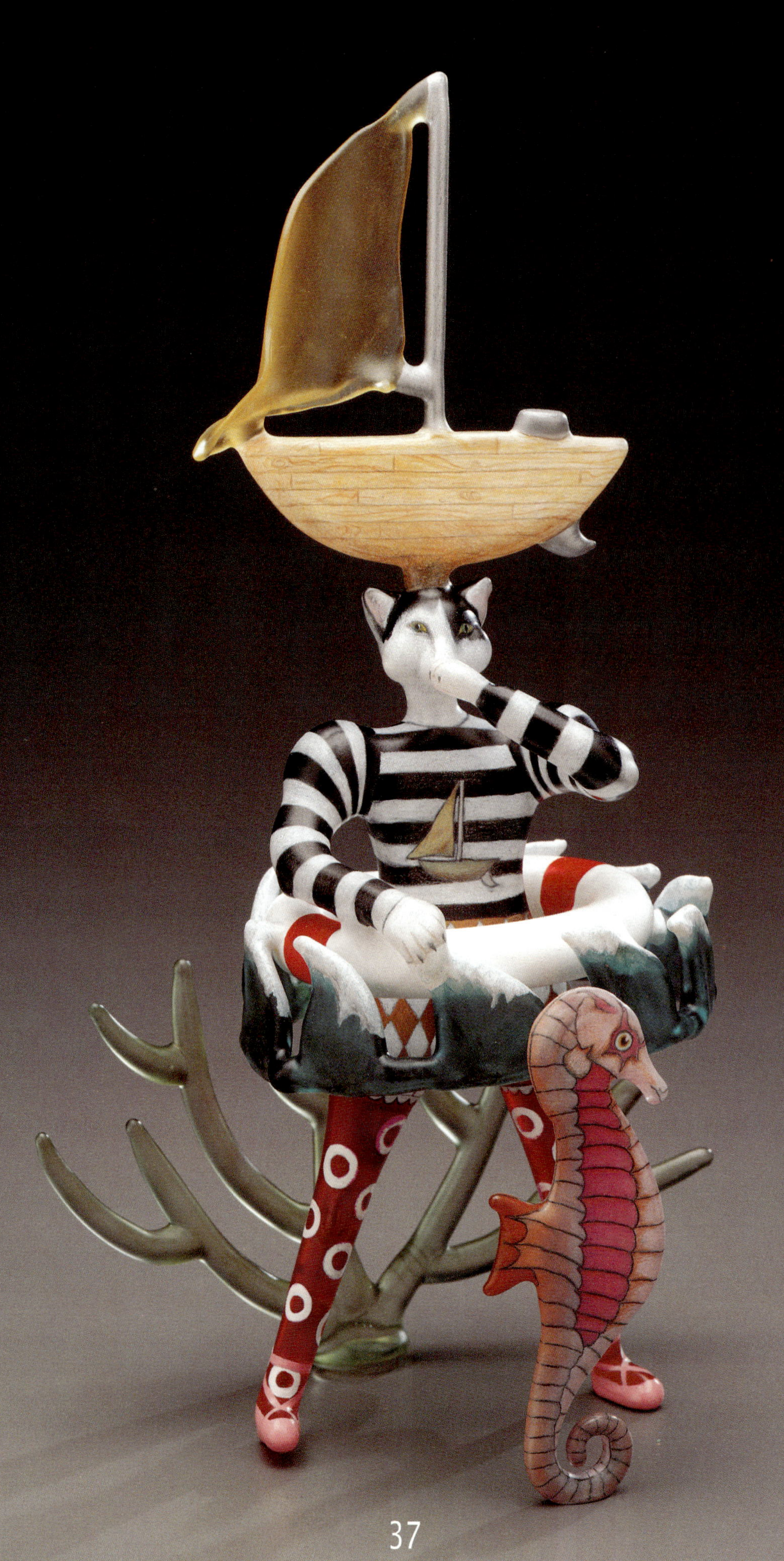

27. **Balance Series: Learning to Cat Paddle**
1995
39.37 x 22.86 x 17. 78
Flameworked glass; mixed media
Lent by Ginny Ruffner

28. **Balance Series: Coping with the Fountain of Youth**
1995
49.53 x 22.86 x 22.86
Flameworked glass; mixed media
Lent by Ginny Ruffner

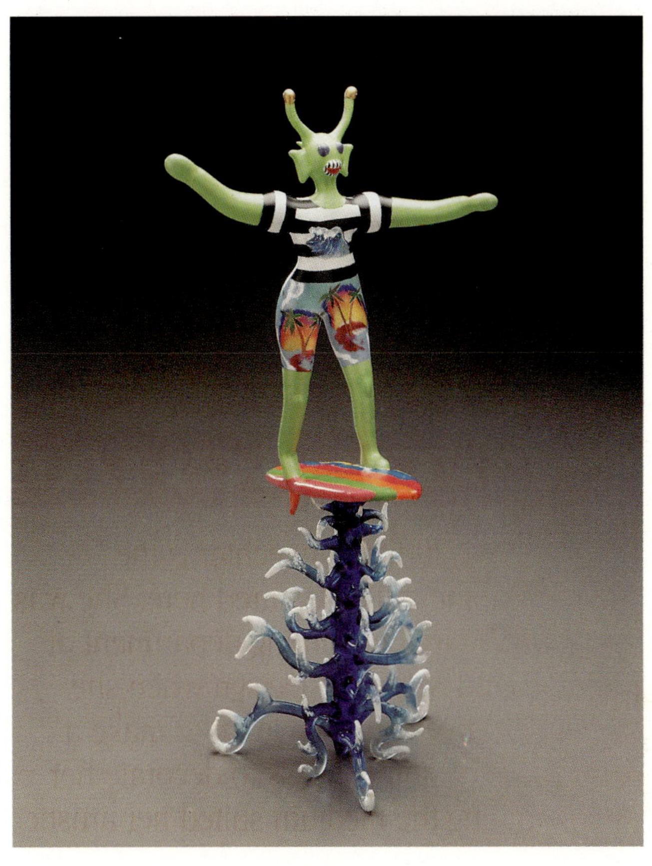

29. **Balance Series: Collaboration**
1995
12.70 x 40.64 x 22.86
Flameworked glass; mixed media
Catalog only; not in exhibition
Courtesy of Ginny Ruffner

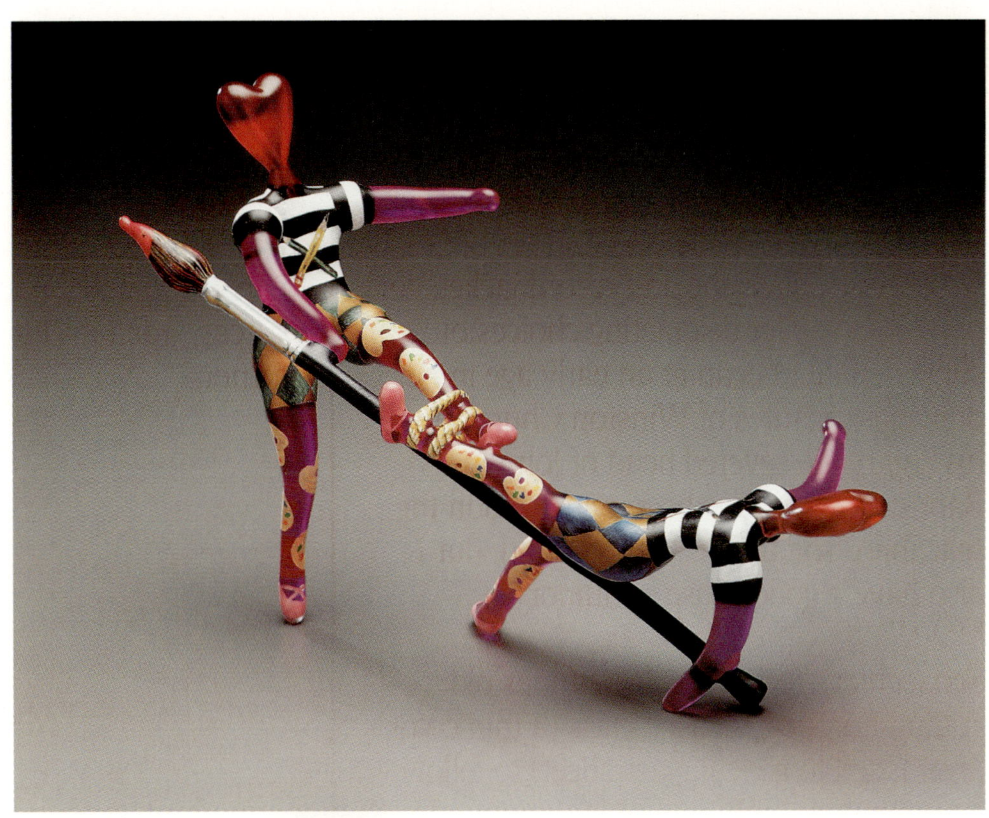

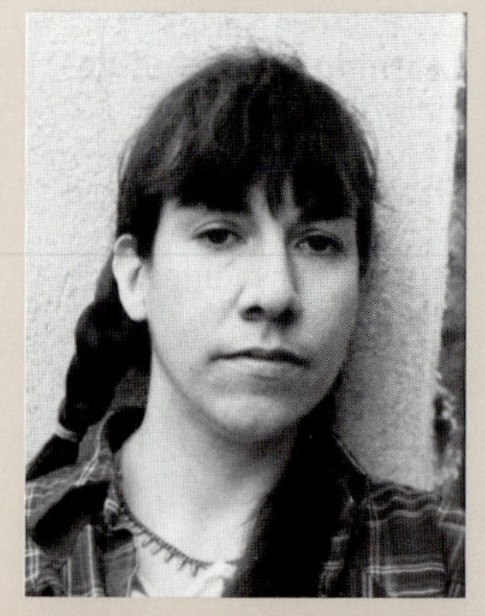

JUDITH SCHAECHTER

Born in 1961, Judith Schaechter is the youngest of the artists featured here. She was a sophomore in the painting department at Rhode Island School of Design when she took an elective course to learn to make a small piece of stained glass to decorate her room. Finding the medium suited her artistic vision, she earned a bachelor of fine arts in glass.

With a painter's eye for imagery, Schaechter combines the beauty of rich color and elaborate detail with scenes of "gruesome beauty" according to one critic. Because of her compelling graphic imagery, she has been given opportunities to create cover art for both *New Yorker* magazine and record jackets for punk bands. Her disquieting choices of subject matter began at an early age in her drawings: pictures of Winston Churchill in his coffin, the severed head of John the Baptist. "I've always been interested in the macabre," she admits. "I'm morbid, but I also have a good sense of humor."

Schaechter's technique is centuries old: cutting European "flash" glass (a thin color layer fused to a clear glass sheet) to follow the image contours of an initial drawing, or "cartoon," then engraving, painting, and firing it to fuse the image to the surface before combining the elements into a panel. However medieval her process, her influences are contemporary. "I watch television—*Star Trek,* detective shows, and *Unsolved Mysteries*—and I sketch a lot while I'm watching. This is actually very important because all the sketches I do while watching TV are uninhibited as I'm paying attention to the TV. Things will start to catch my eye that I end up sketching in an intuitive way.

"I try to be universal. I like sentimental themes like love. And I also try while making the piece to make it as exquisitely beautiful as I can. Idea and technique are equal partners."

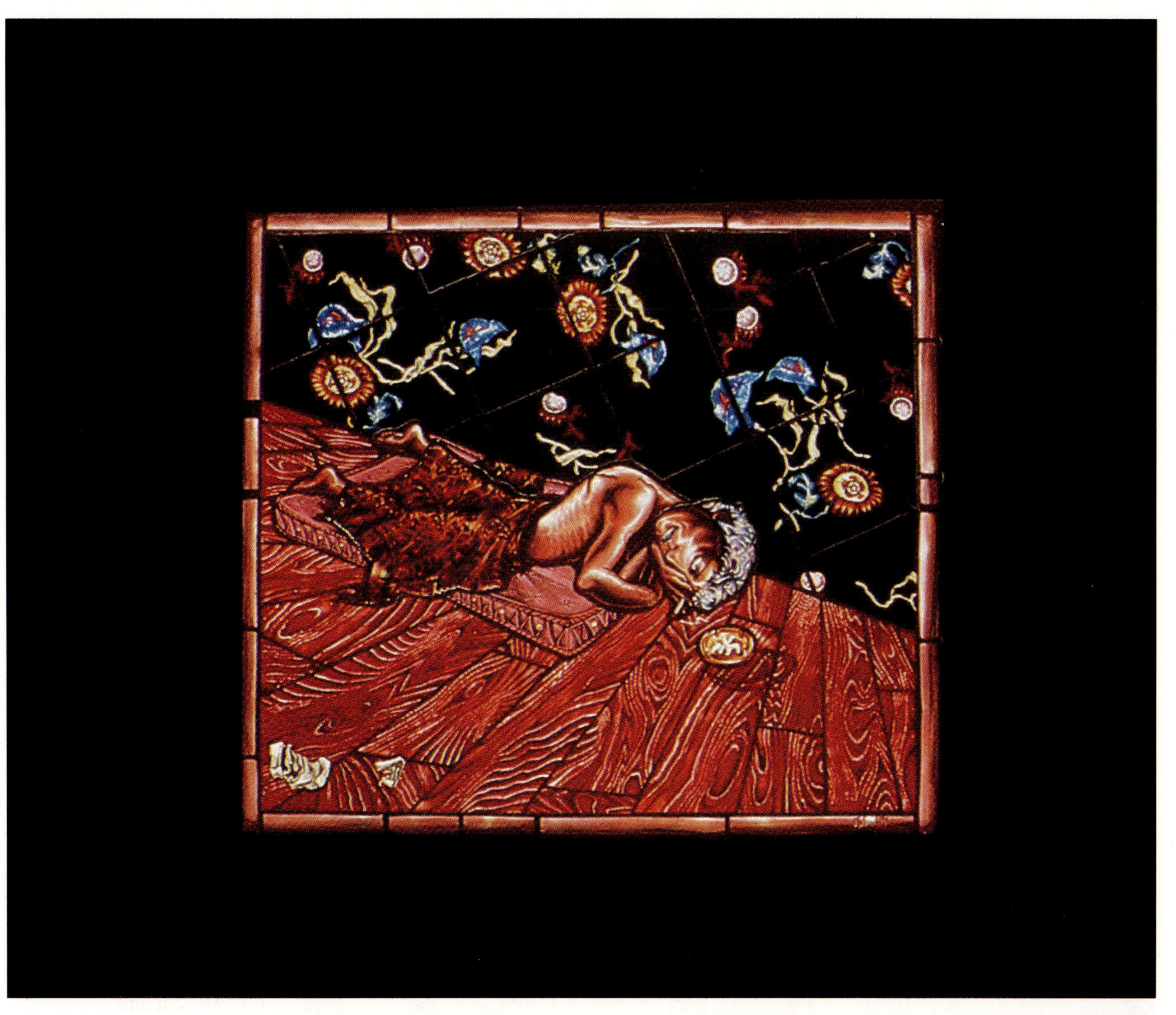

30. **Bad Night with Insomnia**
1994
66.04 x 74.93 x 15.24
Sandblasted, stained and leaded glass
Lent by Hooper and Sharon Nichols, Lake Charles, Louisiana

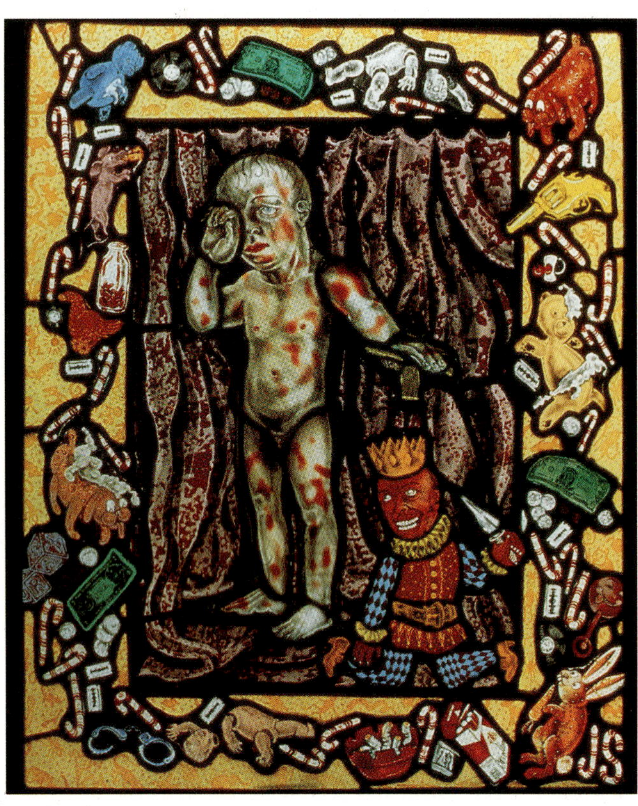

31. **Child and Toy**
1989
58.42 x 48.26 x 15.24
Sandblasted, stained and leaded glass
Lent by Judith Schaechter, courtesy of Snyderman Gallery, Philadelphia, Pennsylvania

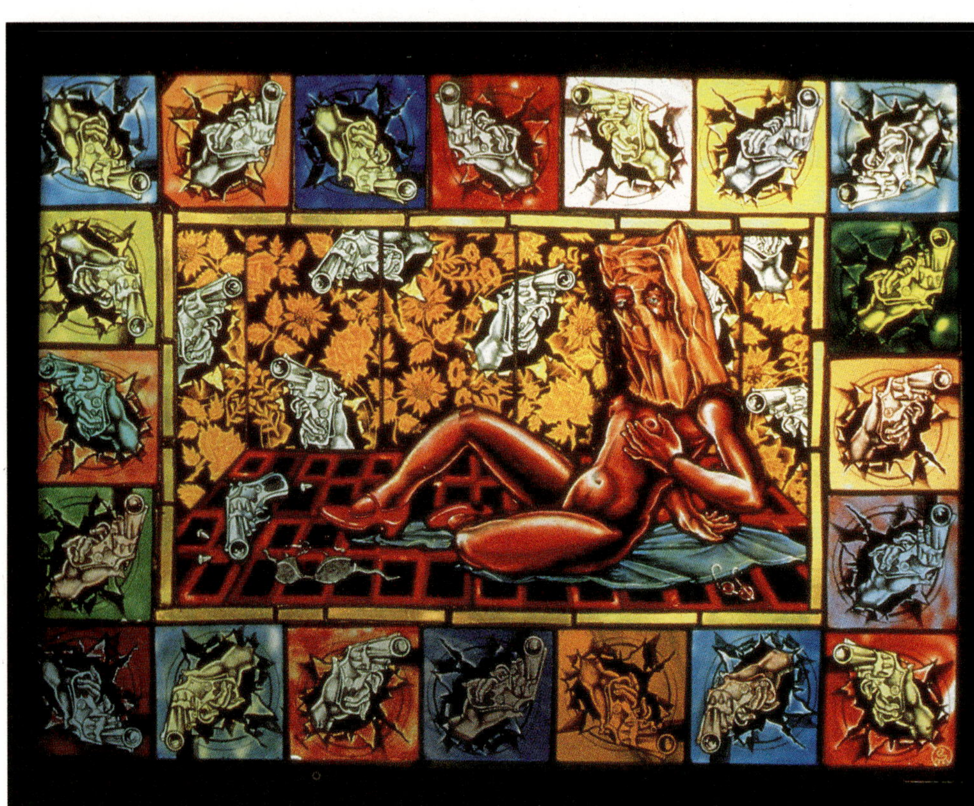

32. **Respecting the Bag**
1992
53.34 x 73.66 x 15.24
Sandblasted, stained and leaded glass
Lent by Paul and Elmerina Parkman

33. **Spilled Life**
1992
53.34 x 68.58 x .63
Colored pencil drawing on paper; photocopy
Catalog only; not in exhibition
Courtesy of Bruce and Marina Kaiser

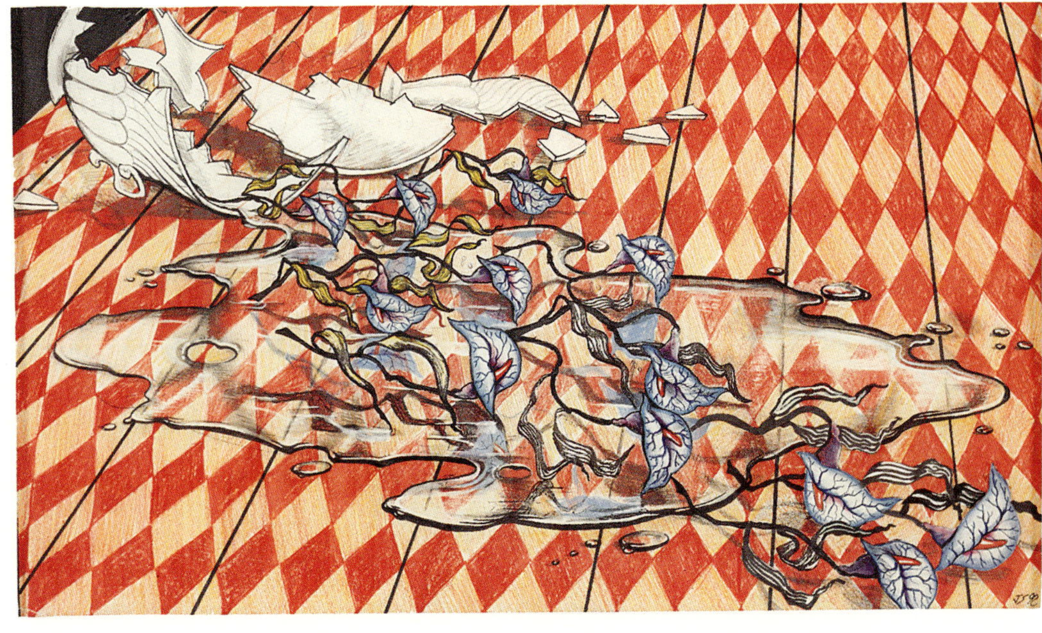

34. **Spilled Life**
1992
50.80 x 76.20 x 15.24
Sandblasted, stained and leaded glass
Lent by Bruce and Marina Kaiser

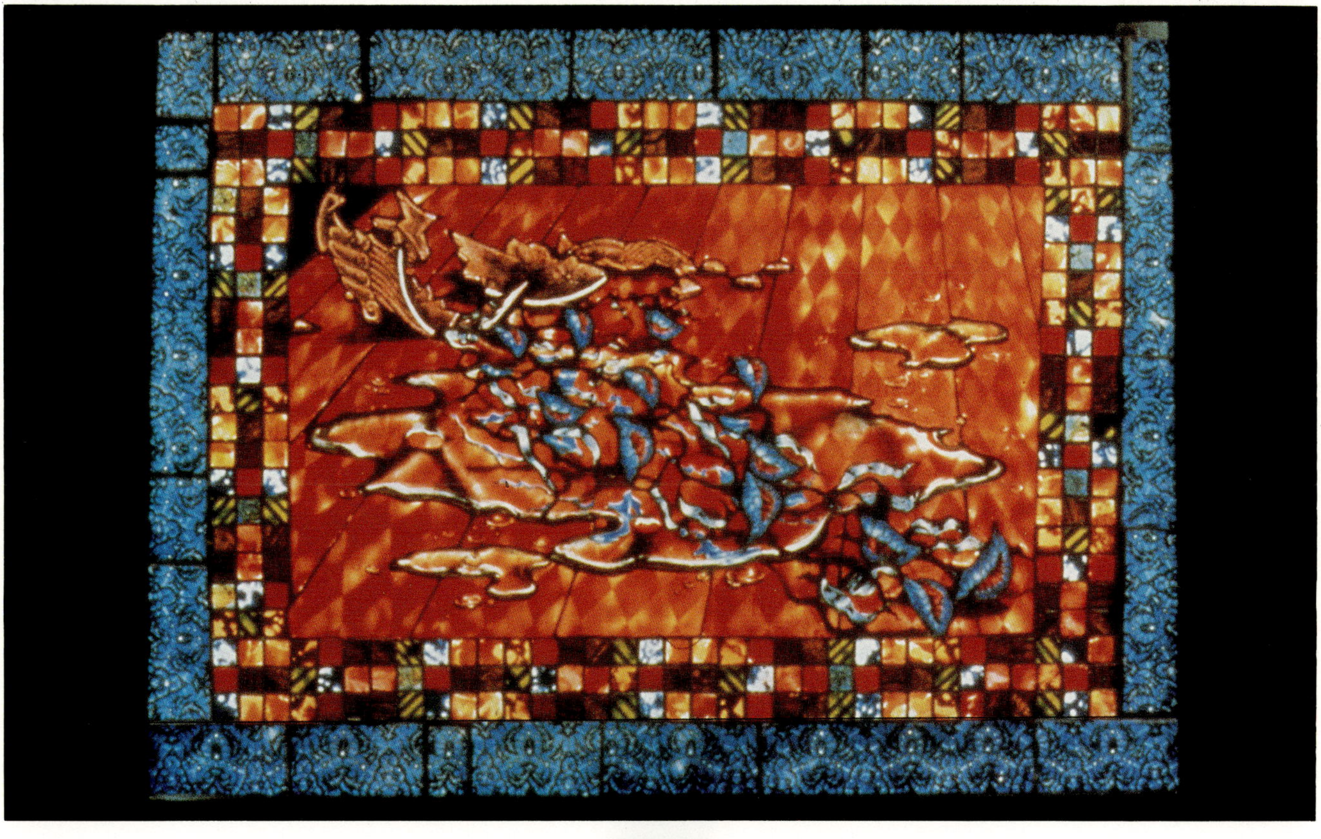

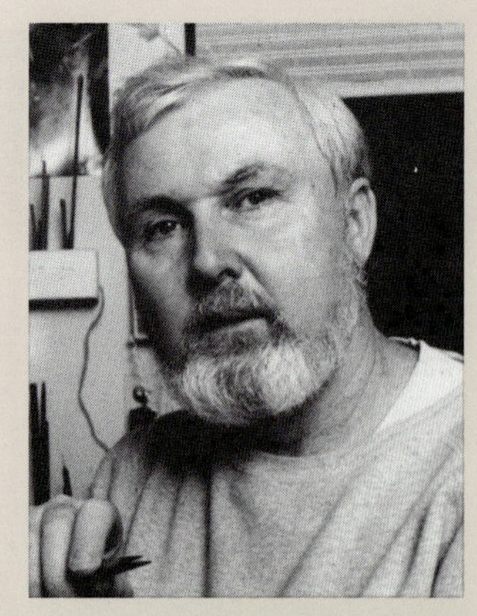

PAUL JOSEPH STANKARD

From the botanical portraits that Paul Stankard created in his early glass paperweights, the artist has progressed to communicating a sublime consciousness of the natural world, even including insects along with several stages of a flower's bloom and decline. Sometimes the gnarled roots of his plants are revealed to be human figures, and occasionally tiny words are imbedded in the glass with them. Words are important, too, to the poet Stankard.

Unique in his precise use of the flameworking (or lampworking) technique, Stankard brings a technical and industrial background to making art. After graduating from a technical college, he was in charge of a scientific glassblowing department at a major research center when he began to experiment making glass paperweights.

Stankard's botanical miniatures extend the tradition of nineteenth-century French paperweights collected for their aesthetic significance, but his glass artistry also evokes the glass botanical models in the Peabody Museum in Massachusetts, which also inspired him. His careful forming, with tweezers, of the delicate petals and stamens in glass may take place indoors—the artist bent over a flame to manipulate the softened glass to his will—but his studio also encompasses the forest of his New Jersey home, where he studies the woodland flowers and other living things that he replicates in glass.

Bridging the technical aspect of his background in glass with the creativity he brings to the medium, the artist acknowledges that he is "building on the modern decorative art tradition, integrating sculptural values. In the contemporary craft world, there are people who respect tradition, who build on it. There are also people who are interested in articulating a whole new format devoid of tradition. In America both positions are well represented. This freedom is one legacy of the studio glass movement."

35. **Autumn's Hour Diptych Botanical**
1993
15.24 x 12.70 x 6.35
Flameworked glass
Lent by Claudia and Wayne Burke

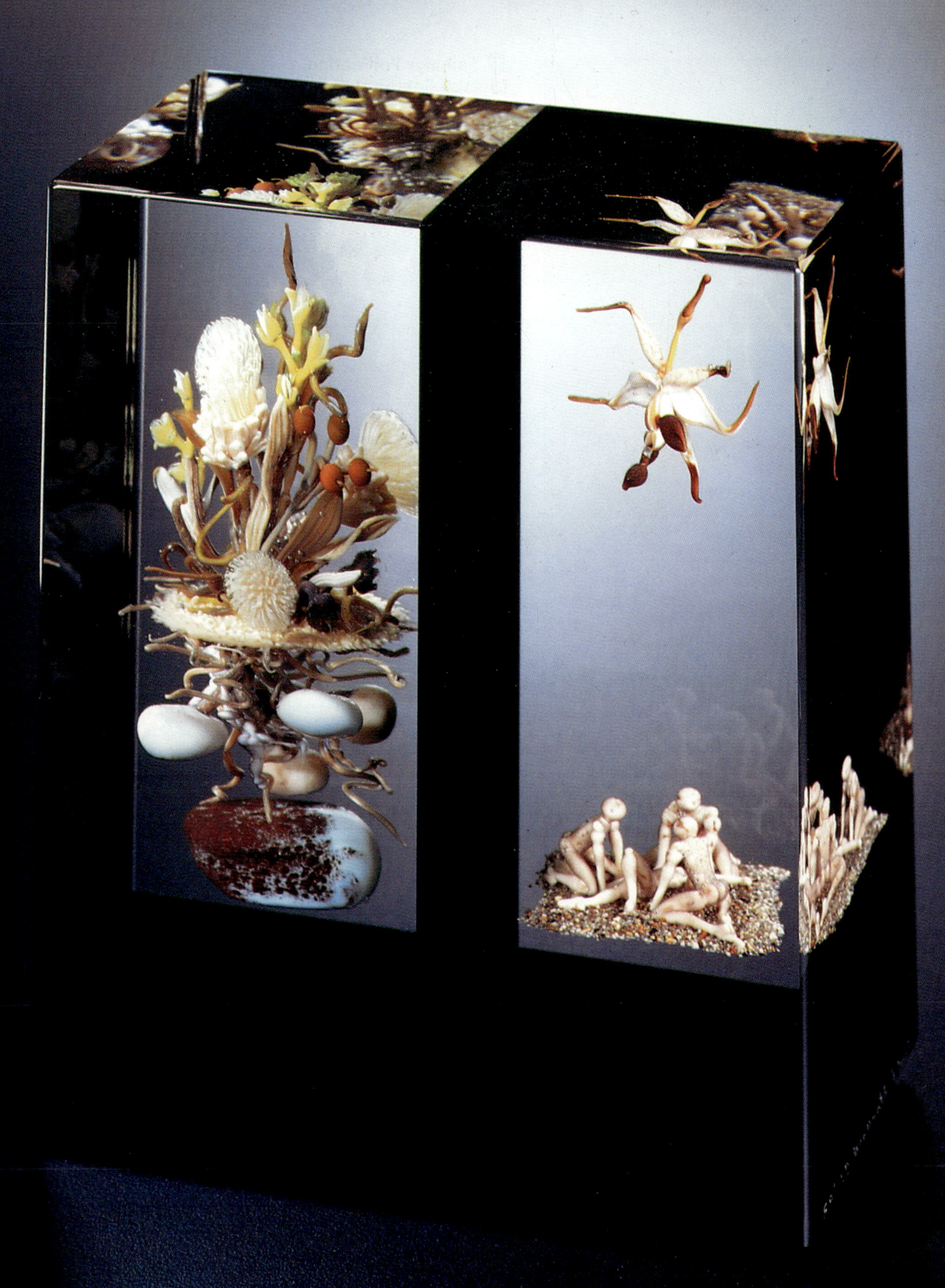

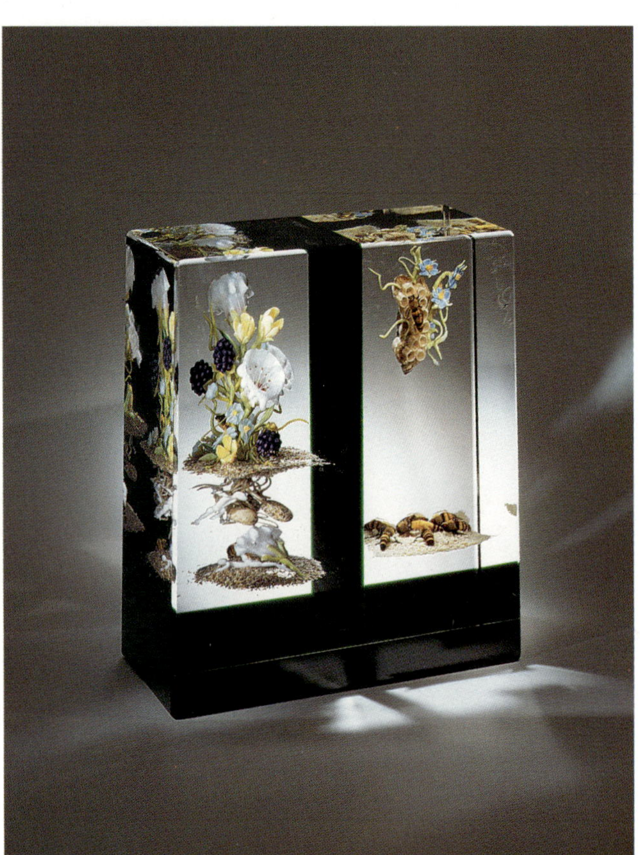

36. **Summer Pollination Diptych Botanical**
1993
15.24 x 12.70 x 5.71
Flameworked glass
Lent by John Halverstam

37. **Summer Assemblage**
1996
17.78 x 20.32 x 12.7
Flameworked glass
James L. Amos photograph
Lent by Mike and Annie Belkin

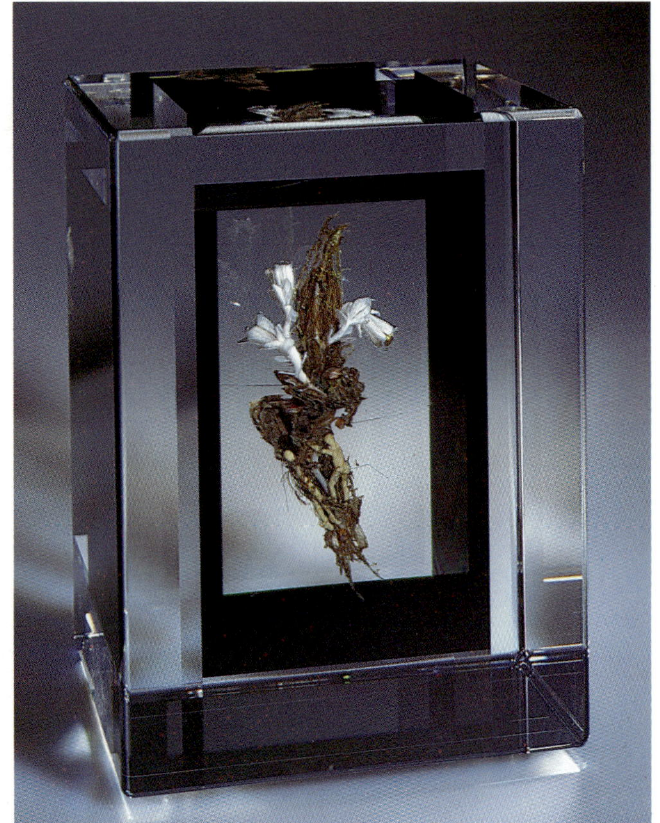

38. **Indian Pipes with Moss Botanical**
1995
16.51 x 16.51 x 7.62
Flameworked glass
Lent by Gary Werths

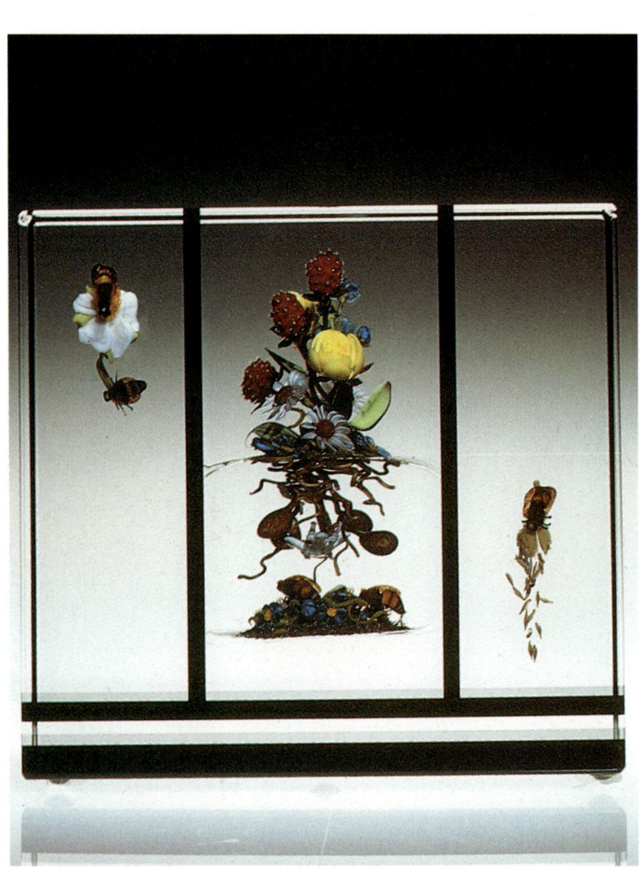

39. **Nature's Continuum Triptych Botanical**
1994
13.97 x 19.35 x 17.46
Flameworked glass
Lent by Daniel and Patricia MacLeith

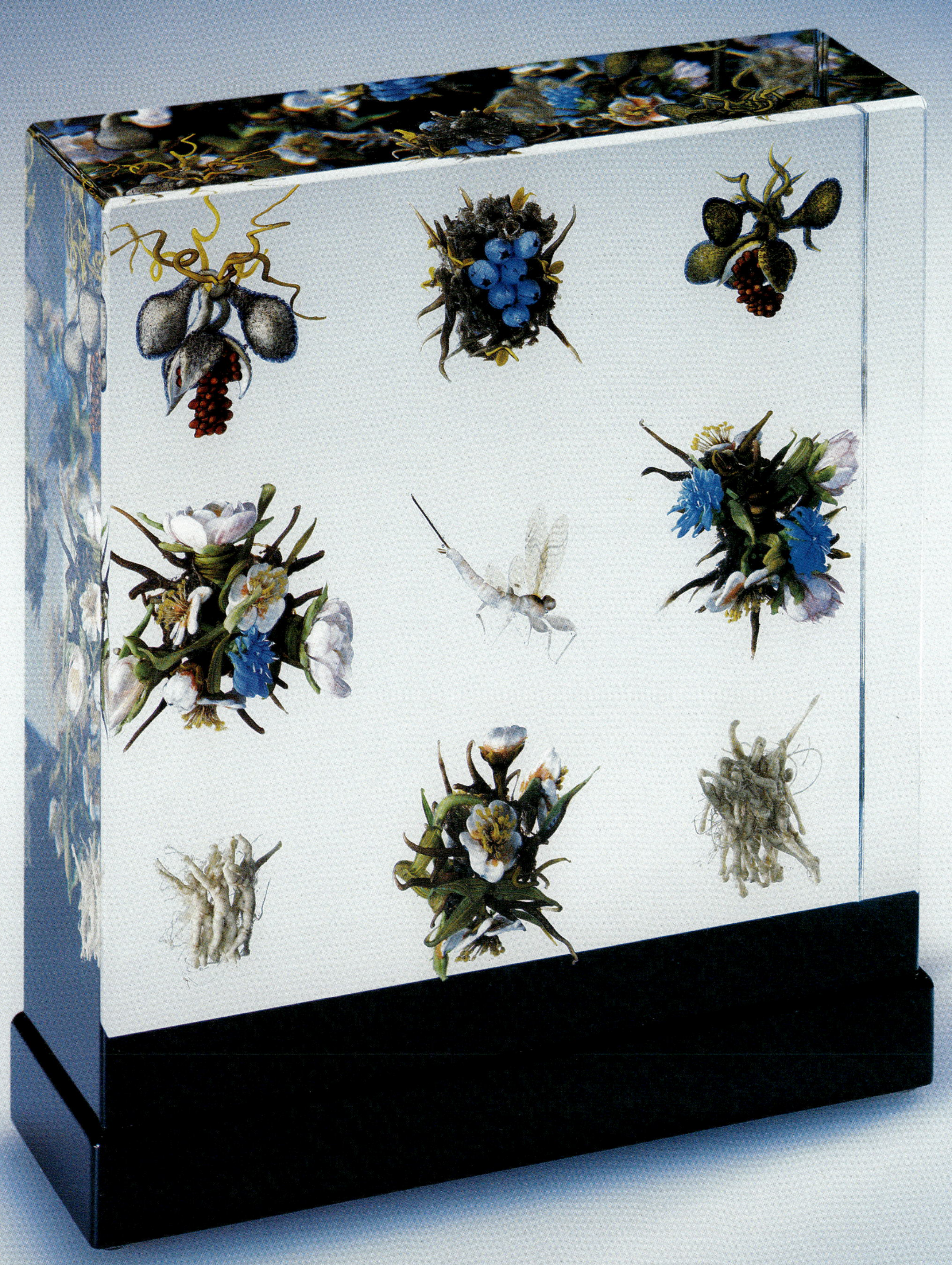

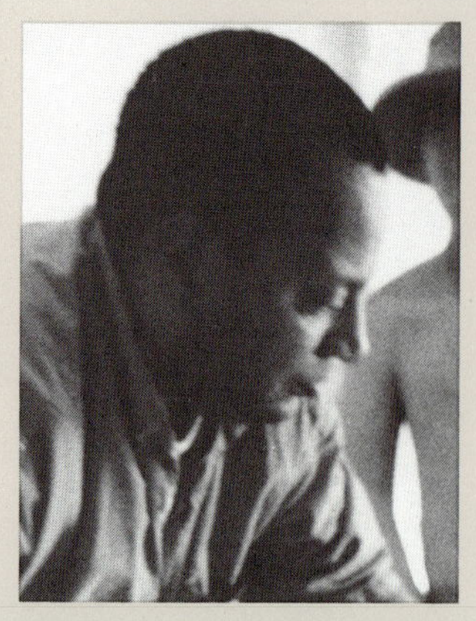

THERMAN STATOM

In recent years Therman Statom, like Dale Chihuly, his former teacher at Rhode Island School of Design, has increasingly made art on an architectural scale. He was commissioned by the city of Los Angeles, where he lives and works, and its transportation system to create art for public places. However, it was necessary to forgo glass and develop his ideas in unfamiliar materials to achieve his distinctive style for both an overhead sculpture in a new subway train station, and three enormous chandeliers for a new wing of the central library.

Since his undergraduate years at Rhode Island School of Design, and at Pratt Institute (New York), where he earned a master of fine arts degree in sculpture, Statom has always been innovative—in material, process, and form. He was among the first artists working in glass to create room-scale installations (some with Richard Marquis). These incorporated both his sculptural forms fabricated from sheets of plate glass and the boldly-brushed paint strokes and applied glass shards and other more disparate objects that modulate the crystalline transparency of the glass and characterize his style.

The installations have generated ideas for smaller works that the artist makes in his studio. His distinctive forms for glass sculpture include chairs, houses, tables, ladders and rectangular boxes ("paintings"). The artist explains that he "consciously limited the studio-generated pieces to five forms...and...the technology of how I make these things and what shapes they are. I'm really interested in the painting and how I develop personal content in the work. A lot of the images have specific symbolic references and implications, but in many cases the reference can be emotionally based rather than having a specific meaning. I have always been interested in my work addressing the intuitive and spiritual side of people."

40. **Maple/Blue Tower**
1995-1996
83.82 x 60.96 x 50.8
Plate glass; enamel paint; mixed media
Lent by Therman Statom, courtesy of Maurine Littleton Gallery, Washington, D.C.

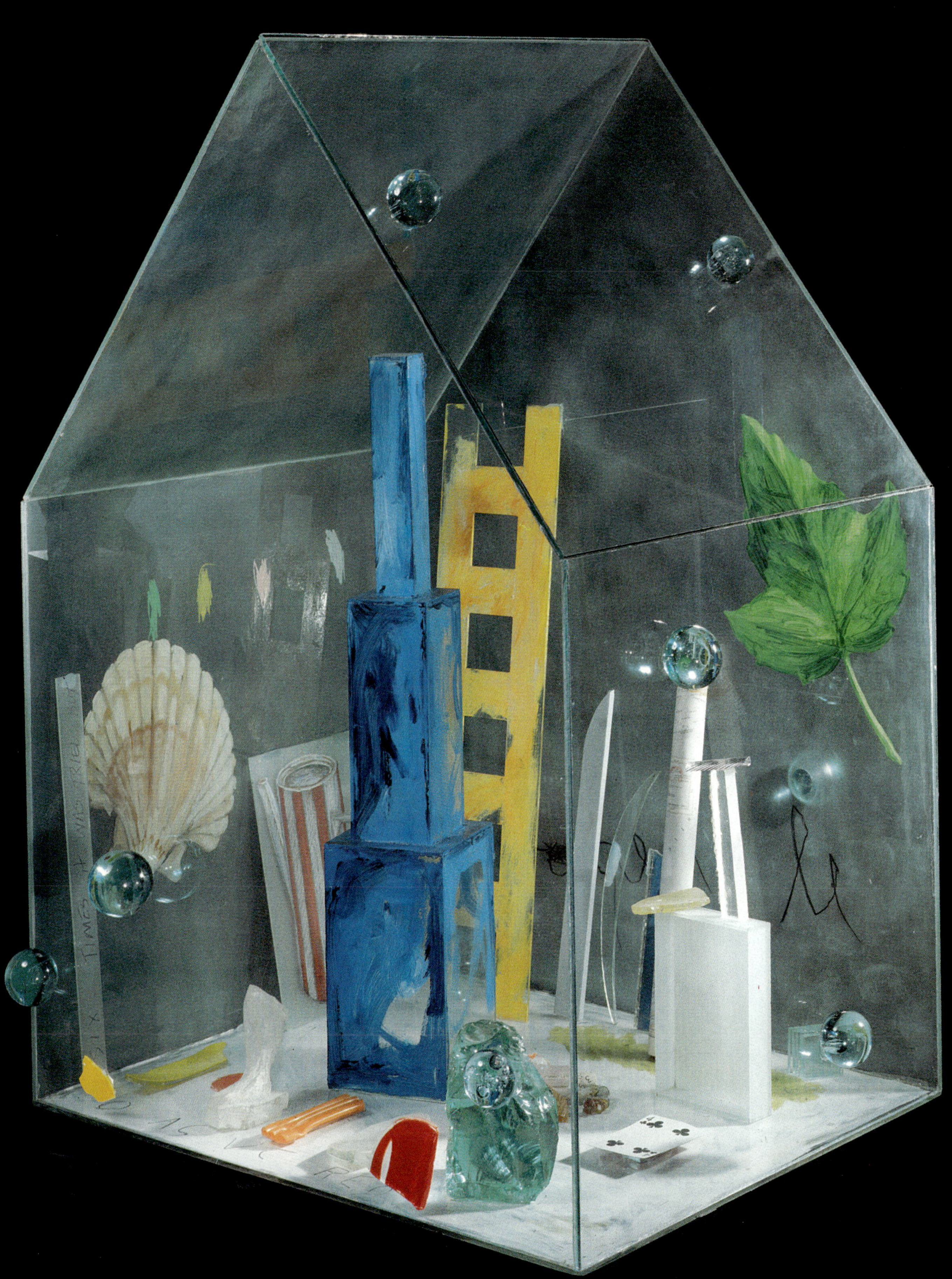

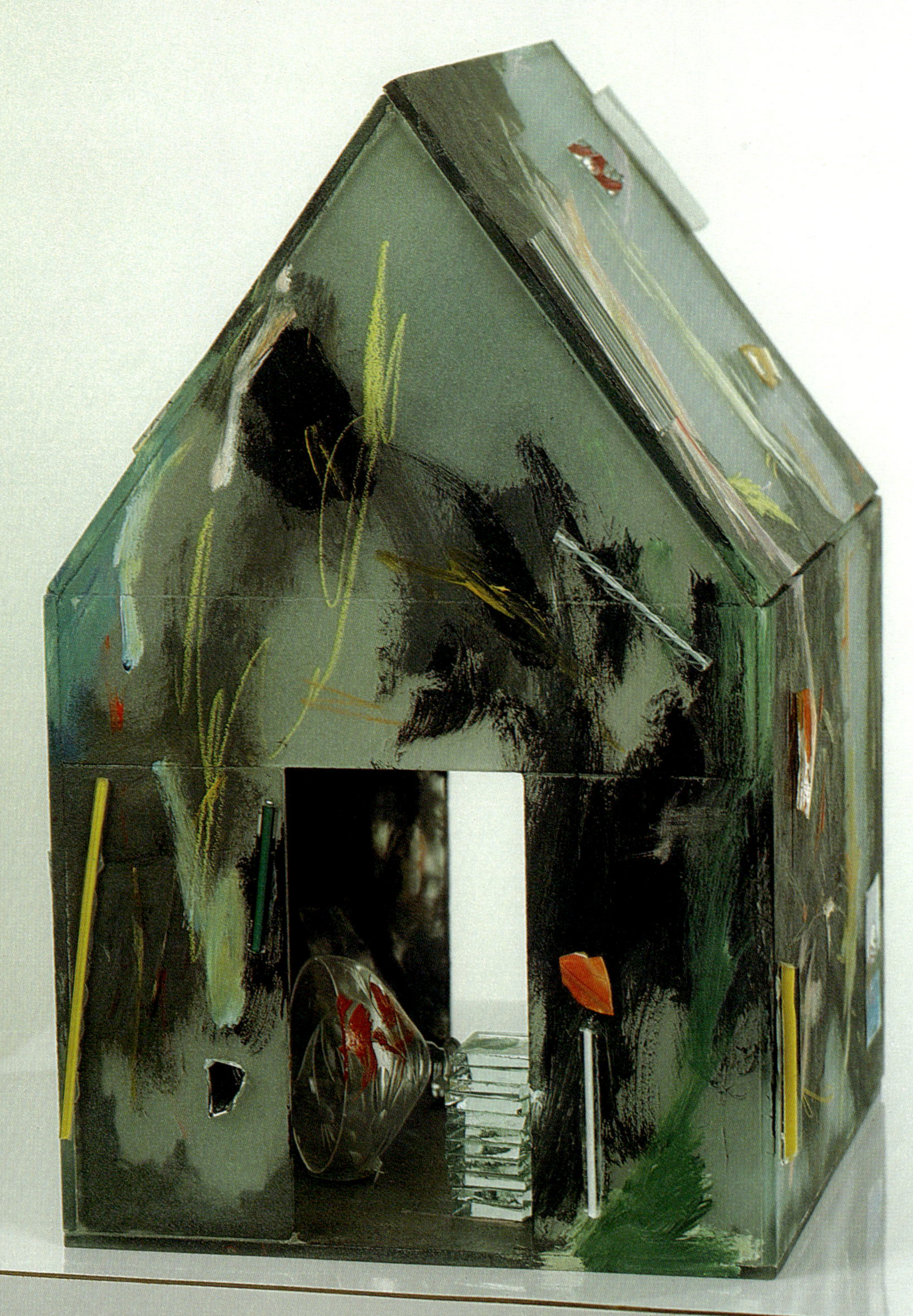

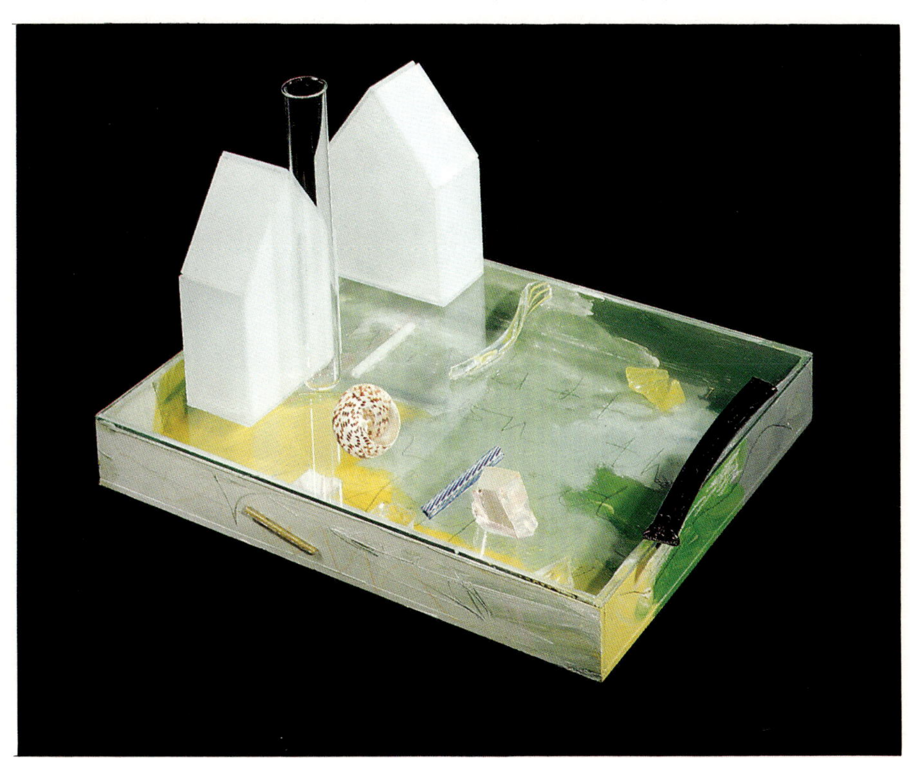

42. **Whyatt**
1996
25.4 x 35.56 x 27.94
Plate glass; enamel paint; mixed media
Lent by Therman Statom, courtesy of Maurine Littleton Gallery, Washington, D.C.

43. **Nine Days/Site**
1996
35.56 x 71.12 x 38.1
Plate glass, enamel paint, mixed media
Lent by Therman Statom, courtesy of Maurine Littleton Gallery, Washington, D.C.

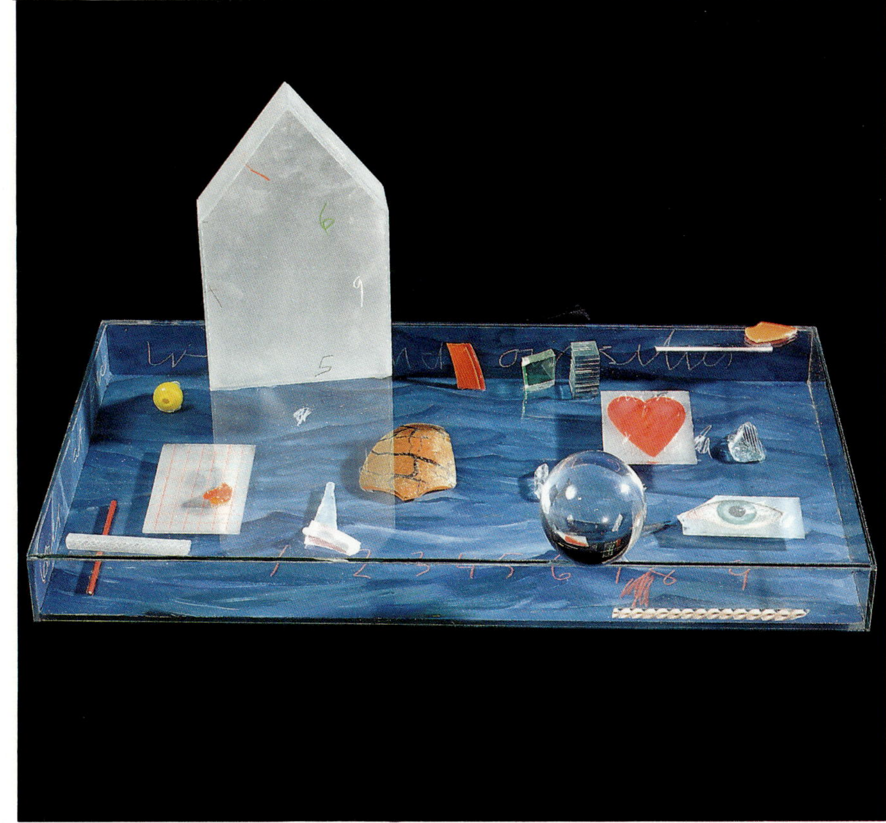

41. **Fallen Glass**
1993
35.56 x 22.86 x 25.40
Plate glass; enamel paint; mixed media
Lent by Therman Statom, courtesy of Maurine Littleton Gallery, Washington, D.C.

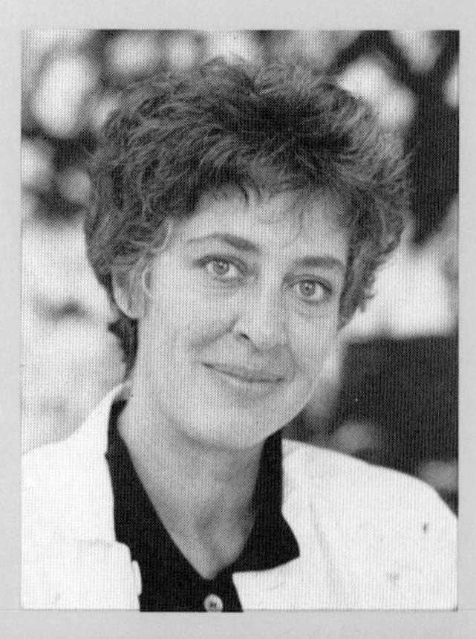

SUSAN STINSMUEHLEN-AMEND

Susan Stinsmuehlen-Amend's evolution has taken her from designing and making stained glass for residences to serving as lead artist on the Hollywood Boulevard Streetscape Team, designing public art in Hollywood, California. Because of the vibrancy of her art, employing glass as only one material in her mixed media sculptures, she is a popular guest artist and lecturer.

Inspired by the universality of much of her personal experience, she says that "Interpretation of my observations is achieved through form and materials. I find the complexities of life are best revealed through mixed media. Accountability for material selection is vital, as each medium brings with it a rich history of associations.

"Remnants" tells a story, but in pieces. Each of the nine panels is a paragraph or episode somewhere in the story. The artist tells us that "the images in each panel are often cut off, as if to hint that there is a bigger story and that you are getting just a piece of it." We remember our experiences in pieces.

"Parts of the story are references to art and recognizing myself as an artist," she reveals. For example, the panel with the white on white rectangle is a glass mosaic homage to the Russian constructivist Kazimer Malevich. Her selection of glass, however, gives extra dimensions and subtle tonalities to her work. Close inspection of the panel brings forth an image of a bird, quite different from the abstractions of Malevich. The art reference has been transformed, just as experiences are transformed in our memories.

While Stinsmuehlen-Amend's work is pictorial, she feels that using glass as her principal medium adds another layer to the meaning of "Remnants." "Glass reflects the real world. But we can also look through it. It both reveals and reflects outside the art. So my use of glass enhances 'Remnants' as a collection of memories brought to the surface as we reflect on our experiences."

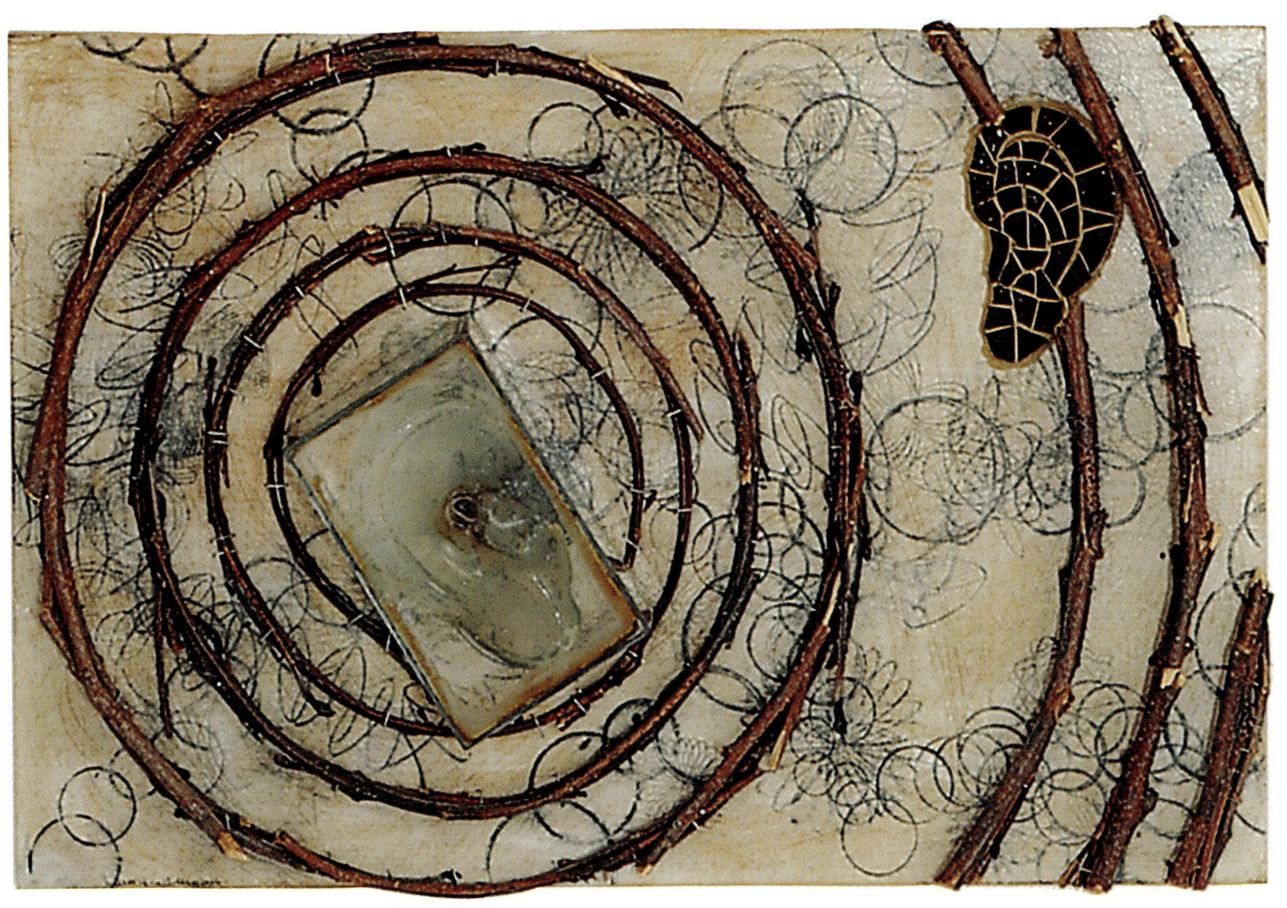

44. **Remnants** *(detail)*
1994

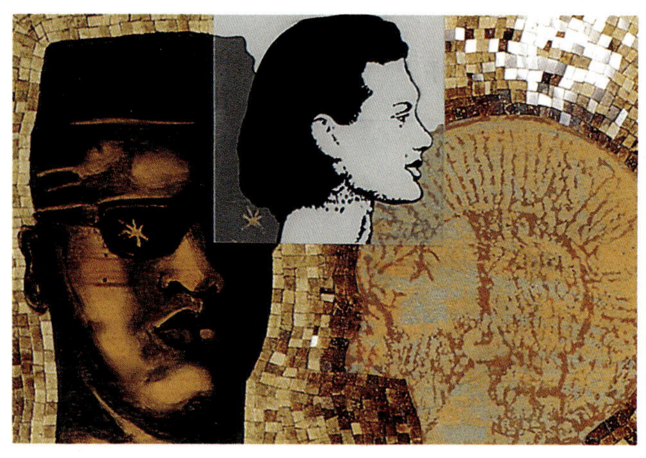
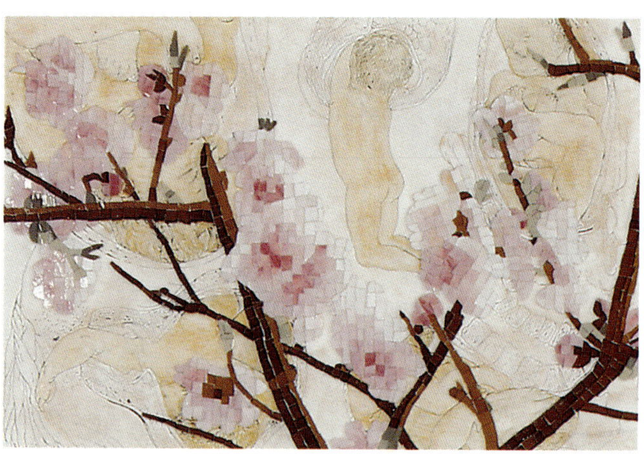
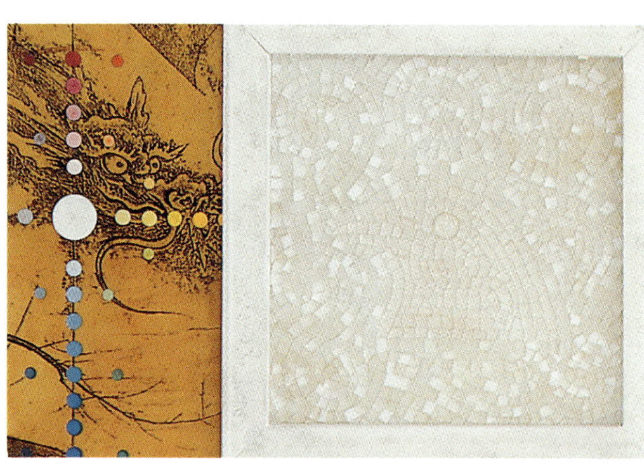
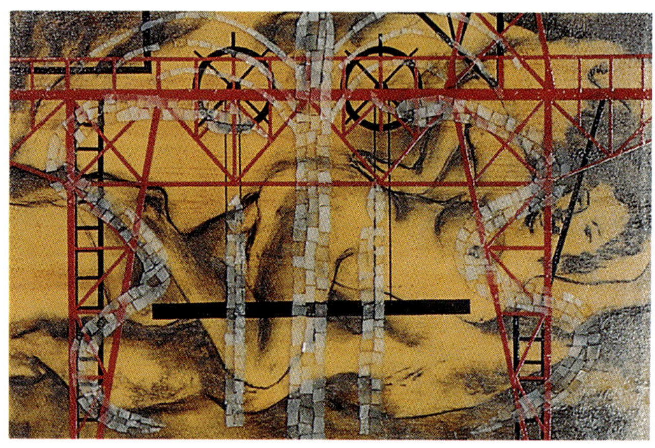
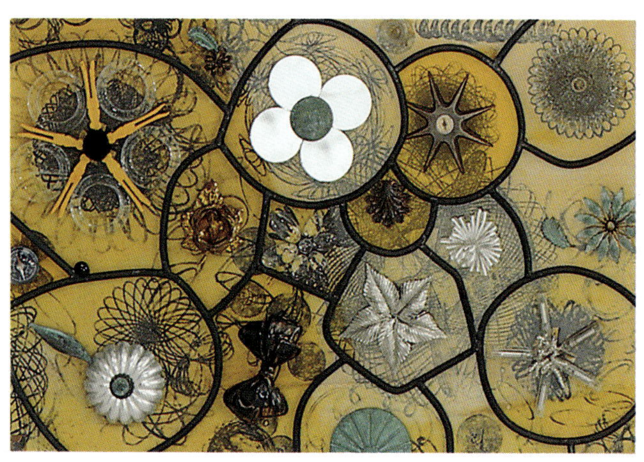
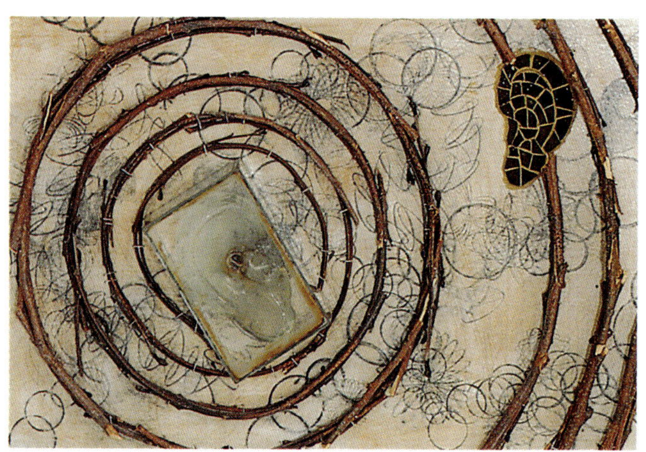

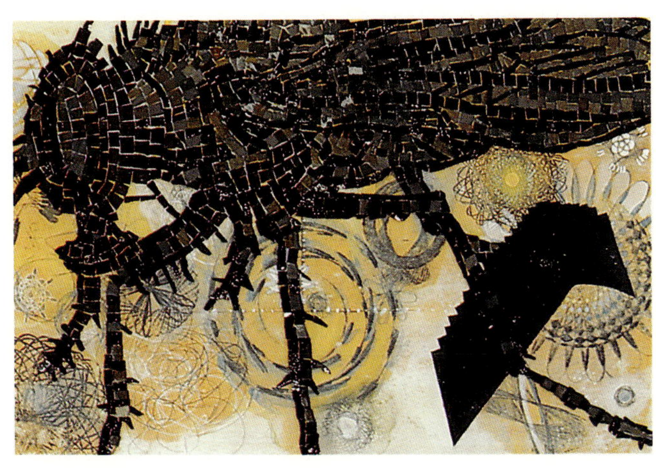

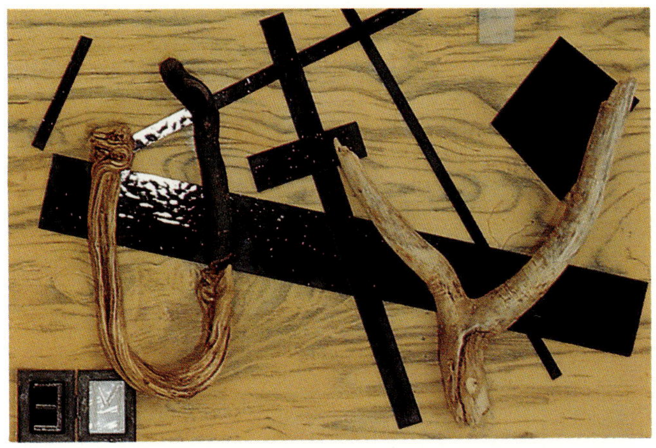

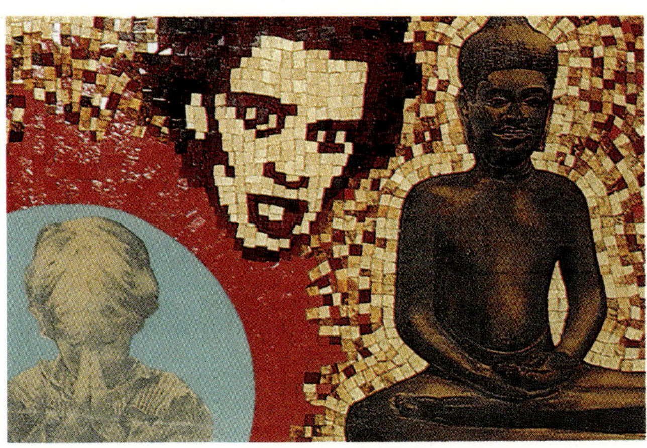

44. **Remnants**
1994
132.08 x 193.04 x 7.62 overall
Sculpted and constructed glass; wood; graphite; mixed media
Lent by Susan Stinsmuehlen-Amend

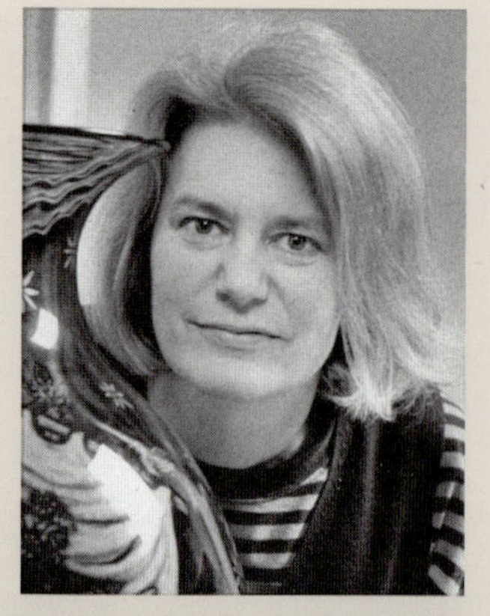

CAPPY THOMPSON

Like many American artists, Cappy Thompson uses the world history of art for inspiration. Her style is strongly influenced by European medieval traditions of painting stained glass windows. When she adapted the pictorial style she developed for windows to the blown glass vessels she paints now, she worked exclusively in *grisaille,* gray tonal painting. Today, she paints in full color, developing imagery in reverse from inside the vessels, which are blown for her by several gaffers in Seattle, Washington, where she lives. Her imaginative scenes, developed in the round, are then fired to fuse the color to the glass surface.

Of the inspiration for her art, she writes: "My work is narrative; sometimes I draw from specific mythologies and folklore, and other times I work more intuitively, building my own narrative in a kind of picture poem based on my imagination and the use of symbols.

"Over the last several years I have made pieces with images of plants and people. These pieces are about relationship, stewardship, love, friendship, work, and celebration. The works themselves are both narrative and symbolic and part of what I enjoy about them is 'reading' them; I like the way the narrative, being inside the vessel, plays with the metaphorical 'world' implied by the vessel form."

In her recent painted scenes Thompson has pictured herself with favorite Hindu deities. Though she is not Hindu, she takes inspiration from the gods and their attributes. "Krishna, who is every artist's dream, being blue, represents spiritual awakening. He is also the lover of every woman and represents awakening to the physical body and loss of shame....*Dancing with Ganesha* is a prayer for moving through obstacles in one's life and about practicing joyfulness," the artist says.

45. **Lord Krishna and Me Standing in the Great Water**
1993
57.15 x 33.02
Blown glass; fired enamel
Michael Seidl photograph
Lent by Cappy Thompson, courtesy of Leo Kaplan Modern, New York, New York

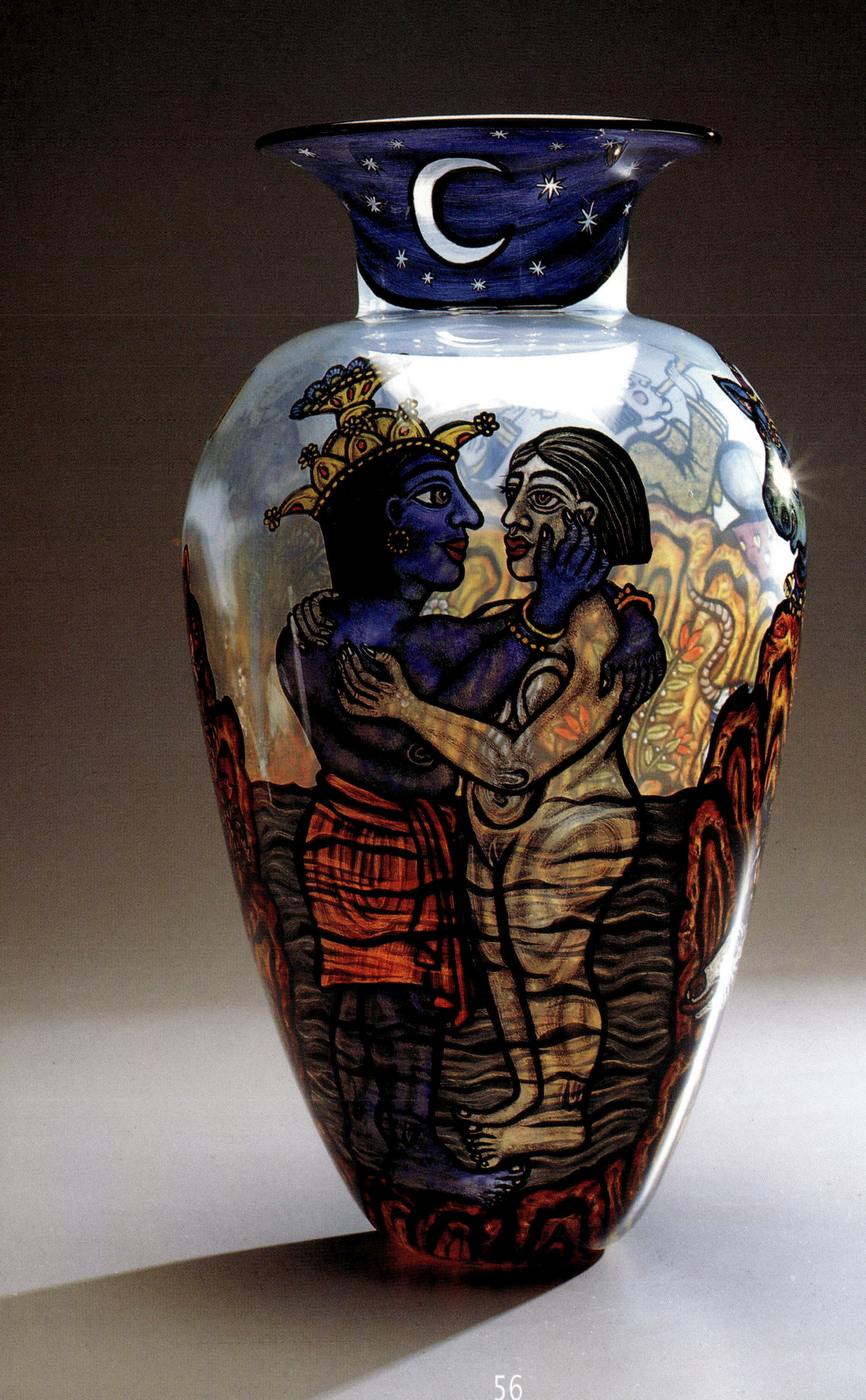

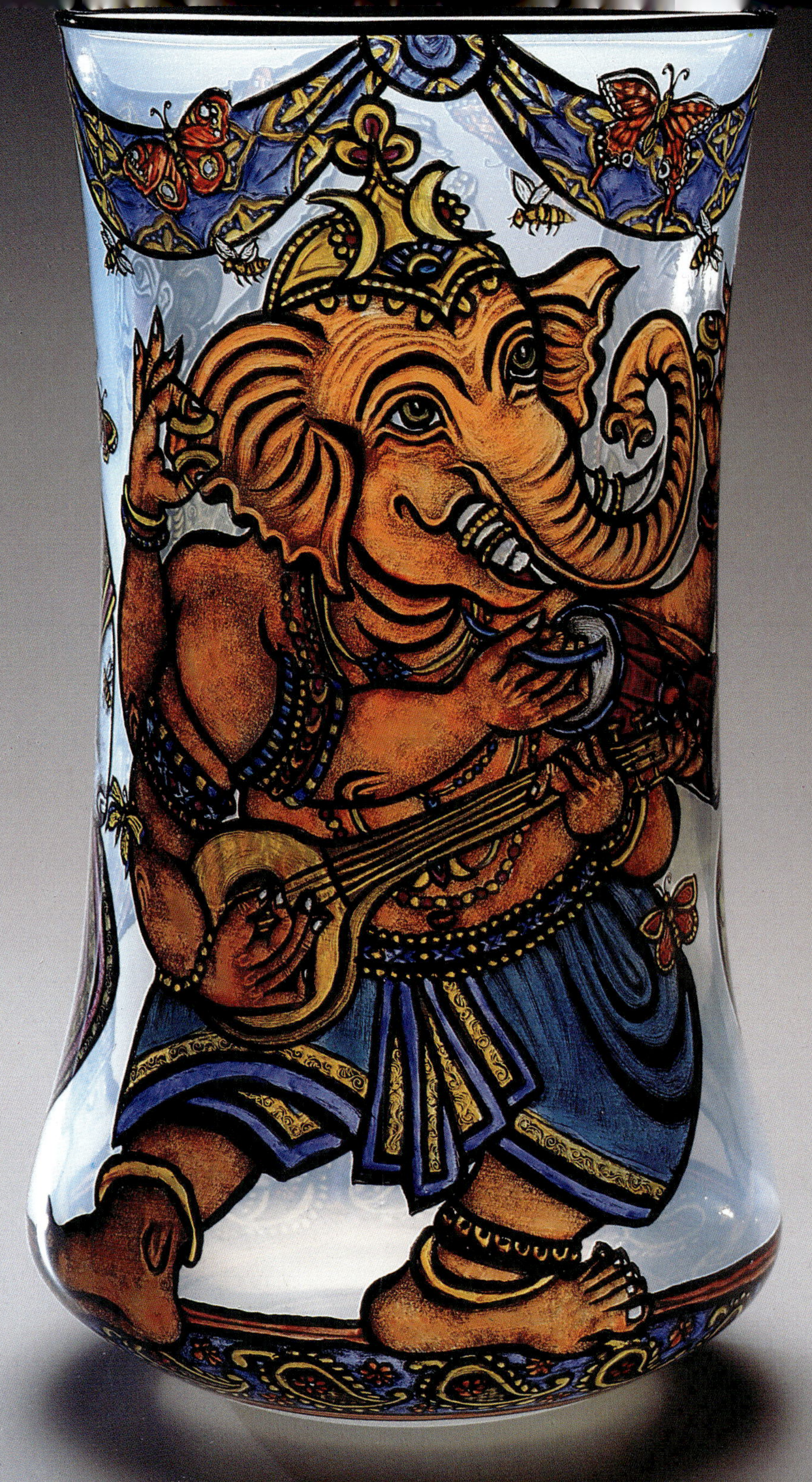

46. **Dancing with Ganesha**
1993
48.26 x 30.48
Blown glass; fired enamel
Michael Seidl photograph
Lent by Cappy Thompson,
courtesy of Leo Kaplan
Modern, New York, New York

47. **My Life With Lord Krishna**
1993
38.10 x 35.56
Blown glass; fired enamel
Lent by Andrea and
Charles Bronfman

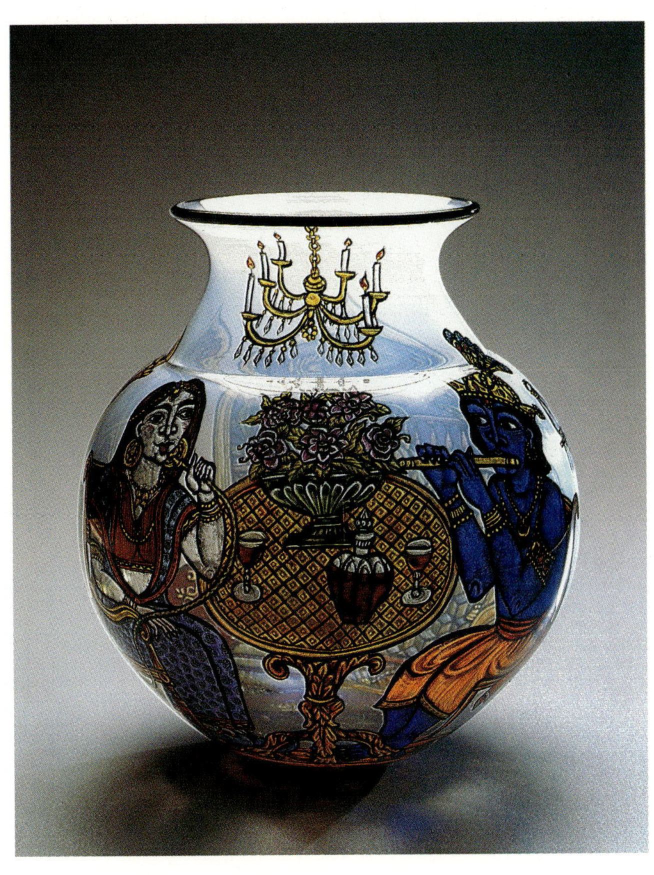

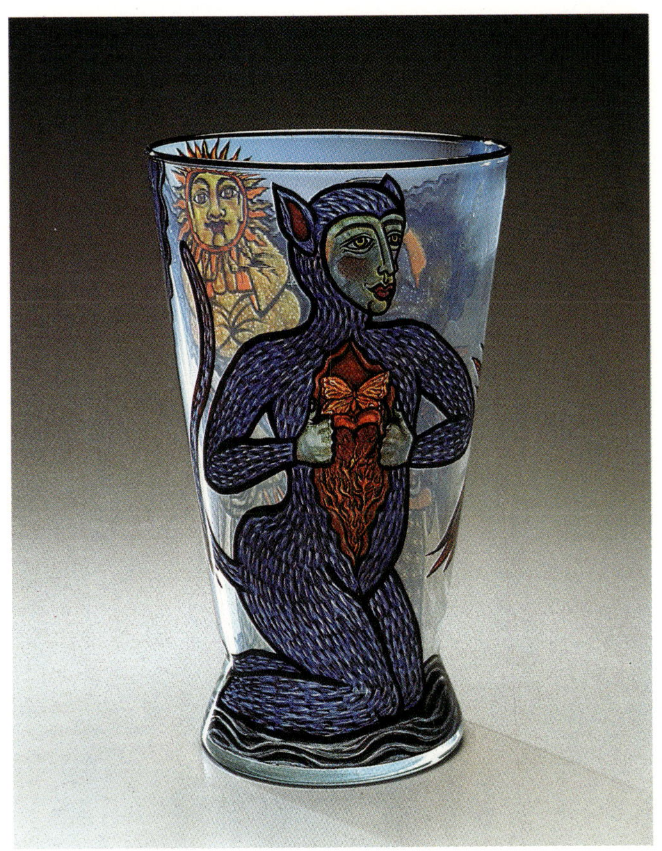

48. **Through my Animal Nature, I am Transformed, in the Altar of my Heart, Assisted by Angels Bearing Gifts from the Sun and the Moon**
1995
44.45 x 26.67
Blown glass; fired enamel
Lent by Cappy Thompson,
courtesy of Leo Kaplan
Modern, New York, New York

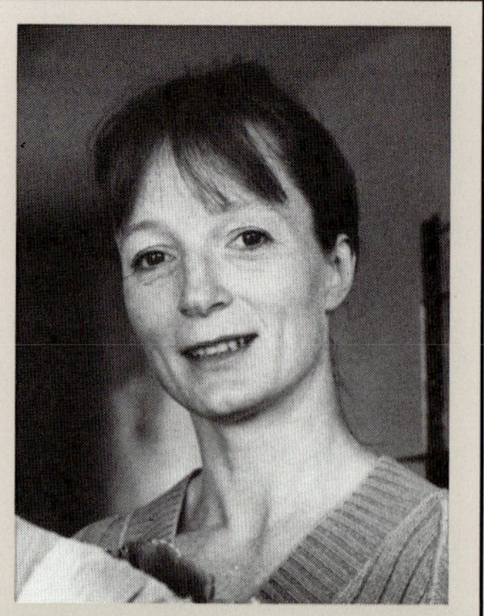

Wouter Thorn Leeson photograph

TOOTS ZYNSKY

An American living in Europe, Toots Zynsky is known by glass aficionados worldwide for her unique process of making sculptural glass bowls and for the glowing colors of her palette. She is a popular teacher and lecturer, and her art has been exhibited more extensively in European nations and Japan than perhaps any other American glass artist.

While studying drawing, painting, and fashion design as a freshman at Rhode Island School of Design, Mary Ann "Toots" Zynsky was introduced to glass as a medium for art. In it she found a new love and created a new technique: wrapping glass threads around blown glass forms to create lustrous layers. It is one of several new techniques she uses but is not represented here.

Fine threads have been applied to decorate glass for centuries, but with the use of equipment made for her by a co-inventor in Amsterdam, Zynsky was able to fuse layers of glass threads to actually form a vessel from them, like those shown. Today she orders colored glass rods from Murano, the Venetian glass center, and after heating them, pulls them into hairlike threads. They are laid flat, layer upon layer of color, heated to 640 degrees Celsius, then manipulated with pizza spatulas and put into a stainless steel bowl to be reheated and shaped.

"It's really like painting," the artist says. "It's an identical thought process—the way you build up a painting or a drawing, and then the other layers go on really to hold that together so it's actually about 30 layers of thread. They are very solid, they look more fragile than they are."

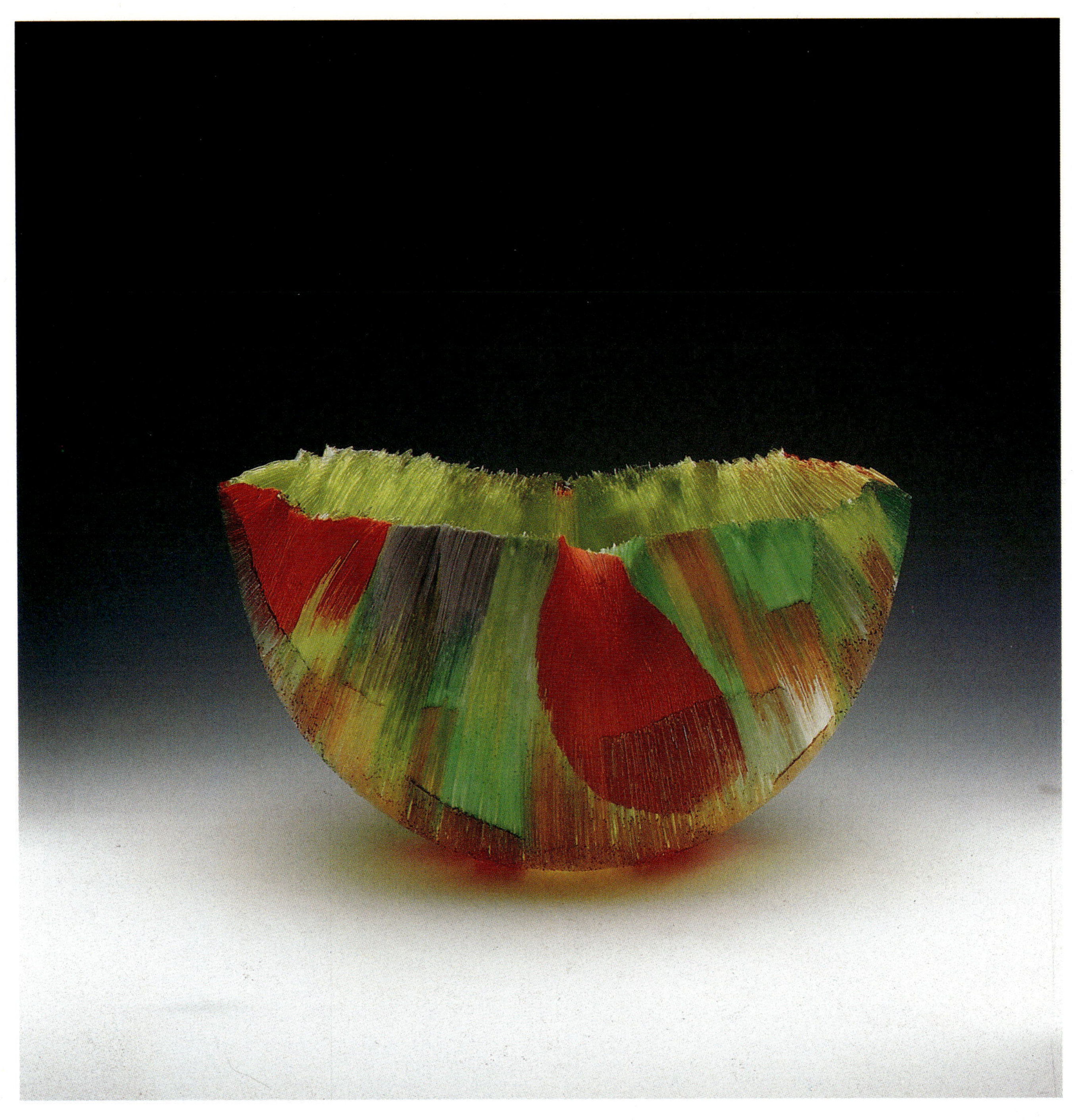

49. **Old Egypt**
1992
16.51 x 29.21 x 29.21
Extruded glass threads, fused
Lent by Toots Zynsky and Elliott Brown Gallery, Seattle, Washington

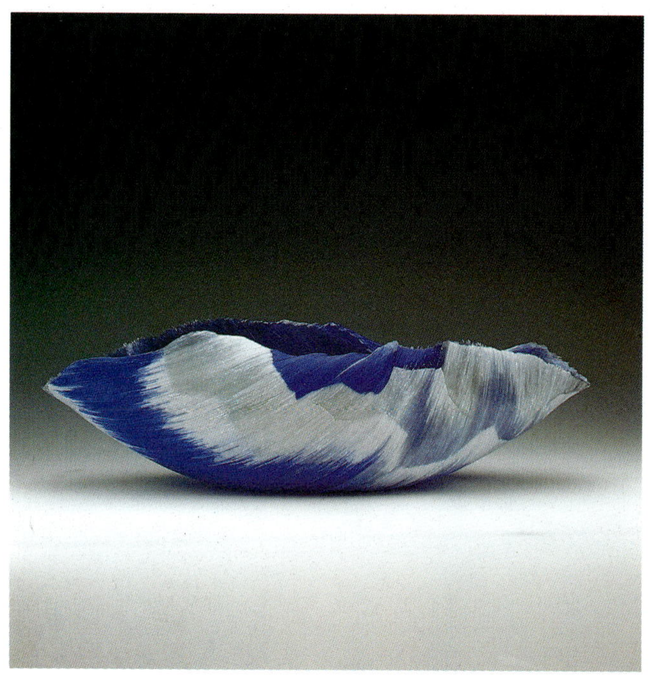

50. **Icebergs II**
1992
13.33 x 45.38 x 18.41
Extruded glass threads, fused
Lent by Toots Znysky and Elliott Brown Gallery, Seattle, Washington

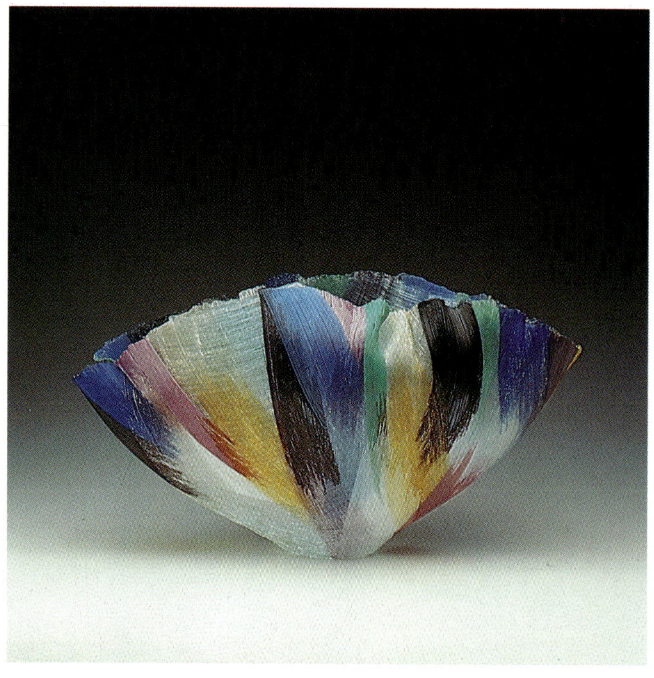

51. **Light Chaos II**
1995
16.51 x 31.75 x 16.51
Extruded glass threads, fused
Lent by Toots Zynsky and Elliott Brown Gallery, Seattle, Washington

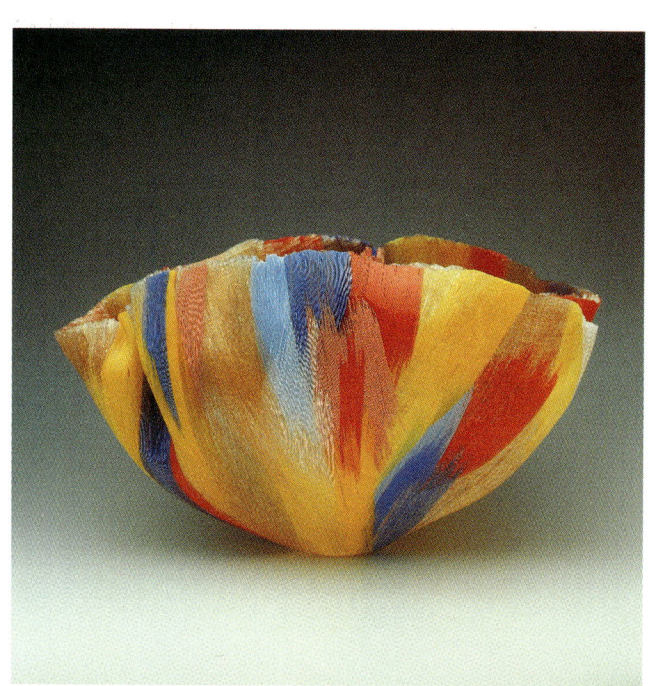

52. **Positive Chaos**
1995
19.05 x 33.02 x 21.59
Extruded glass threads, fused
Lent by Toots Zynsky and Elliott Brown Gallery, Seattle, Washington

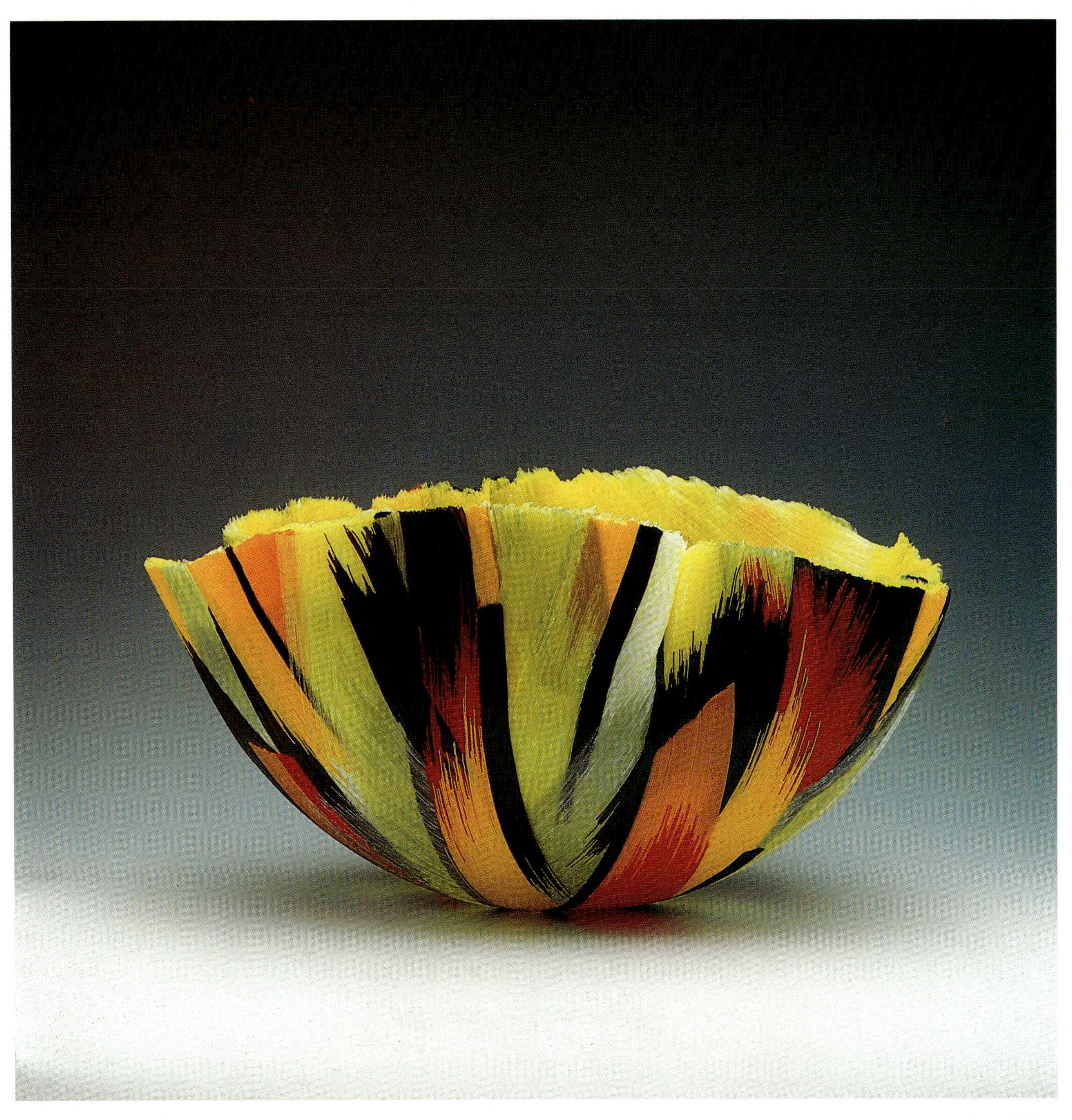

53. **City Lights**
1993
17.14 x 33.02 x 21.59
Extruded glass threads,
fused
Lent by Toots Zynsky and
Elliott Brown Gallery, Seattle,
Washington

Checklist of the Exhibition

DALE CHIHULY

1. **Gilded Rose Venetian with Chartreuse Green Coil**
1990
60.96 x 40.64 x 38.10
Blown and sculpted glass
Claire Garoutte photograph
Lent by Dale Chihuly

2. **Pink Venetian**
1990
38.10 x 43.18 x 40.64
Blown and sculpted glass
Roger Schreiber photograph
Lent by Dale Chihuly

3. **Gold over Prussian Blue Venetian**
1990
111.76 x 35.56 x 33.02
Blown and sculpted glass
Claire Garoutte photograph
Lent by Dale Chihuly

4. **Cadmium Yellow Venetian with Umber Flowers**
1991
73.66 x 43.18 x 40.64
Blown and sculpted glass
Claire Garoutte photograph
Lent by Dale Chihuly

DAN DAILEY

5. **Puff**
1992
52.07 x 38.10
Blown and sculpted glass
Lent by Dan Dailey

6. **Haute**
1991
63.50 x 27.94
Blown and sculpted glass
Lent by Dan Dailey

7. **Foreign**
1991
57.15 x 27.94
Blown and sculpted glass
Lent by Dan Dailey

8. **Serenity**
1994
58.42 x 33.02
Blown and sculpted glass
Lent by Dan Dailey

MICHAEL GLANCY

9. **Crystal Obscura**
Base 1986; Object 1998
15.24 x 20.32 x 38.1
Blown glass; industrial plate glass; silver; copper
Gene Dwiggins photograph
Lent by Daniel Greenberg and Susan Steinhauser

10. **The Still Point**
1991
35.56 x 45.72 x 45.72
Blown glass; industrial plate glass; copper
Lent by the artist, courtesy of Galerie von Bartha, Basel, Switzerland

11. **Tricolored Cohesian**
1994
21.59 x 19.05 x 19.05
Blown glass; copper; silver and gold
Lent by Daniel Greenberg and Susan Steinhauser

RICHARD MARQUIS

12. **Coffeepot Sample Box**
1993-94
48.83 x 30.48 x 9.84
Blown glass; mixed media
Rob Vinnedge photograph
Lent by Kate Elliott, Elliot Brown Gallery, Seattle, Washington

13. **Teapot Goblet**
1990
27.94 x 10.16 x 8.89
Blown glass
Rob Vinnedge photograph
Lent by Kate Elliott, Elliot Brown Gallery, Seattle, Washington

14. **Teapot Goblet #219**
1990
26.67 x 10.16 x 8.25
Blown glass
Rob Vinnedge photograph
Lent by Arthur Liu

15. **Teapot Goblet 94-12**
1994
20 x 14.28
Blown glass
Rob Vinnedge photograph
Lent by Arthur Liu

16. **Teapot Box #3**
1993
14.60 x 52.07 x 10.16
Blown glass; mixed media
Rob Vinnedge photograph
Lent by Arthur Liu

WILLIAM MORRIS

17. **Canopic Jar: Buck**
1992
104.14 x 30.48
Blown and sculpted glass
Rob Vinnedge photograph
Lent by Gary Werths

18. **Canopic Jar: Dahl Sheep**
1994
91.44 x 50.80 x 38.10
Blown and sculpted glass
Rob Vinnedge photograph
Lent by George R. Stroemple Collection, Portland, Oregon

19. **Canopic Jar: Gazelle**
1995
132.08 x 30.48
Blown and sculpted glass
Rob Vinnedge photograph
Lent by George R. Stroemple Collecion, Portland, Oregon

20. **Canopic Jar: Hawk**
1995
68.58 x 25.4
Blown and sculpted glass
Rob Vinnedge photograph
Lent by William Morris

THOMAS PATTI

21. **Red Lumina with Compound Disk**
1991
10.31 x 14.12 x 9.98
Fused, hand-shaped, ground and polished glass
Lent by the Patti Collection, Plainfield, Massachusetts

22. **Black Echo with Green**
1992
10.16 x 15.87 x 11.43
Fused, hand-shaped, ground and polished glass
Lent by the Patti Collection, Plainfield, Massachusetts

23. **Green Lumina Echo with Red**
1993
12.36 x 14.27 x 11.09
Fused, hand-shaped, ground and polished glass
Lent by the Patti Collection, Plainfield, Massachusetts

24. **Starfire Lumina with Blue, Green, Red and Mirrorized Disk**
1994
10.31 x 15.06 x 11.32
Fused, hand-shaped, ground and polished glass
Lent by the Patti Collection, Plainfield, Massachusetts

25. **Spectral Starphire Clear with Mirrorized Disk, Orange and Black**
1994-95
11.02 x 14.90 x 10.79
Fused, hand-shaped, ground and polished glass
Lent by the Patti Collection, Plainfield, Massachusetts

GINNY RUFFNER

26. **Balance Series: The Container and the Contained**
1994
48.26 x 33.02 x 22.86
Flameworked glass; mixed media
Lent by Ginny Ruffner

27. **Balance Series: Learning to Cat Paddle**
1995
39.37 x 22.86 x 17. 78
Flameworked glass; mixed media
Lent by Ginny Ruffner

28. **Balance Series: Coping with the Fountain of Youth**
1995
49.53 x 22.86 x 22.86
Flameworked glass; mixed media
Lent by Ginny Ruffner

29. **Balance Series: Collaboration**
1995
12.70 x 40.64 x 22.86
Flameworked glass; mixed media
Catalog only; not in exhibition
Lent by Ginny Ruffner

JUDITH SCHAECHTER

30. **Bad Night with Insomnia**
1994
66.04 x 74.93 x 15.24
Sandblasted, stained and leaded glass
Lent by Hooper and Sharon Nichols, Lake Charles, Louisiana

31. **Child and Toy**
1989
58.42 x 48.26 x 15.24
Sandblasted, stained and leaded glass
Lent by Judith Schaechter, courtesy of Snyderman Gallery, Philadelphia, Pennsylvania

32. **Respecting the Bag**
1992
53.34 x 73.66 x 15.24
Sandblasted, stained and leaded glass
Lent by Paul and Elmerina Parkman

33. **Spilled Life**
1992
53.34 x 68.58 x .63
Colored pencil drawing on paper; photocopy
Catalog only; not in exbition
Lent by Bruce and Marina Kaiser

34. **Spilled Life**
1992
50.80 x 76.20 x 15.24
Sandblasted, stained and leaded glass
Lent by Bruce and Marina Kaiser

PAUL JOSEPH STANKARD

35. **Autumn's Hour Diptych Botanical**
1993
15.24 x 12.70 x 6.35
Flameworked glass
Lent by Claudia and Wayne Burke

36. **Summer Pollination Diptych Botanical**
1993
15.24 x 12.70 x 5.71
Flameworked glass
Lent by John Halverstam

37. **Summer Assemblage**
1996
17.78 x 20.32 x 12.7
Flameworked glass
James L. Amos photograph
Lent by Mike and Annie Belkin

38. **Indian Pipes with Moss Botanical**
1995
16.51 x 16.51 x 7.62
Flameworked glass
Lent by Gary Werths

39. **Nature's Continuum Triptych Botanical**
1994
13.97 x 19.35 x 17.46
Flameworked glass
Lent by Daniel and Patricia MacLeith

THERMAN STATOM

40. **Maple/Blue Tower**
1995-1996
83.82 x 60.96 x 50.8
Plate glass; enamel paint; mixed media
Lent by Therman Statom, courtesy of Maurine Littleton Gallery, Washington, D.C.

41. **Fallen Glass**
1993
35.56 x 22.86 x 25.40
Plate glass; enamel paint; mixed media
Lent by Therman Statom, courtesy of Maurine Littleton Gallery, Washington, D.C.

42. **Whyatt**
1996
25.4 x 35.56 x 27.94
Plate glass; enamel paint; mixed media
Lent by Therman Statom, courtesy of Maurine Littleton Gallery, Washington, D.C.

43. **Nine Days/Site**
1996
35.56 x 71.12 x 38.1
Plate glass; enamel paint; mixed media
Lent by Therman Statom, courtesy of Maurine Littleton Gallery, Washington, D.C.

SUSAN STINSMUEHLEN-AMEND

44. **Remnants**
1994
132.08 x 193.04 x 7.62 overall
Sculpted and constructed glass; wood; graphite; mixed media
Lent by Susan Stinsmuehlen-Amend

CAPPY THOMPSON

45. **Lord Krishna and Me Standing in the Great Water**
1993
57.15 x 33.02
Blown glass; fired enamel
Michael Seidl photograph
Lent by Cappy Thompson, courtesy of Leo Kaplan Modern, New York, New York

46. **Dancing with Ganesha**
1993
48.26 x 30.48
Blown glass; fired enamel
Michael Seidl photograph
Lent by Cappy Thompson, courtesy of Leo Kaplan Modern, New York, New York

47. **My Life With Lord Krishna**
1993
38.10 x 35.56
Blown glass; fired enamel
Lent by Cappy Thompson, courtesy of Leo Kaplan Modern, New York, New York

48. **Through my Animal Nature, I am Transformed, in the Altar of my Heart, Assisted by Angels Bearing Gifts from the Sun and the Moon**
1995
44.45 x 26.67
Blown glass; fired enamel
Lent by Cappy Thompson, courtesy of Leo Kaplan Modern, New York, New York

TOOTS ZYNSKY

49. **Old Egypt**
1992
16.51 x 29.21 x 29.21
Extruded glass threads, fused
Lent by Toots Zynsky and Elliott Brown Gallery, Seattle, Washington

50. **Icebergs II**
1992
13.33 x 45.38 x 18.41
Extruded glass threads, fused
Lent by Toots Zynsky and Elliott Brown Gallery, Seattle, Washington

51. **Light Chaos II**
1995
16.51 x 31.75 x 16.51
Extruded glass threads, fused
Lent by Toots Zynsky and Elliott Brown Gallery, Seattle, Washington

52. **Positive Chaos**
1995
19.05 x 33.02 x 21.59
Extruded glass threads, fused
Lent by Toots Zynsky and Elliott Brown Gallery, Seattle, Washington

53. **City Lights**
1993
17.14 x 33.02 x 21.59
Extruded glass threads, fused
Lent by Toots Zynsky and Elliott Brown Gallery, Seattle, Washington

Acknowledgments

About the Curator

Lloyd E. Herman is one of the foremost authorities on the contemporary crafts movement in the United States of America. From 1971 until 1986 he served as founding director of the national craft museum of the United States, the Smithsonian Institution's Renwick Gallery in Washington, D.C. He is currently Acting Senior Curator of the International Glass Museum, a new facility opening in Tacoma, Washington during the summer of 2001. He continues to write about American crafts, and organizes exhibitions for circulation by museums and traveling exhibition services. He lives in Seattle, Washington.

About the Project Staff

American Glass: Masters of the Art was originally designed for a European tour under the auspices of the United States Information Agency (USIA). We wish to extend thanks to the original project staff, including Susan Flynt-Stirn and Catherine Williamson of USIA, and Pamela J. Brunton and W. Joseph Gagnon of Seattle, Washington. A special thanks goes to Evangeline J. Montgomery for bringing the exhibition to the attention of the Smithsonian Institution Traveling Exhibition Service (SITES).

We also wish to thank Bob Mahiques, Terry Sullivan, and Mark C. Lundi of USIA for their continued involvement in the production and printing of this catalog. Phil Kovacevich of Seattle, Washington designed the exhibition panels and labels, and Artech, also of Seattle, packed and crated the exhibition for tour.

At SITES, the support of all members of the staff has been generosity itself. Special appreciation goes to the Exhibition Registrar, Viki Possoff, and Head Registrar, Lee Williams. Thanks also to Johleen Cannon, Margi Corsello, Betsy Hennings, Marlene Rothacker, Martha Sewell, Gail Spilsbury, Andrea Stevens, Betty Teller, Fredric Williams, and SITES Director, Anna R. Cohn.

Don Hudgins, Peach Duffy, Holle Simmons, Cornelia Moynihan, Ian Monroe, and Dianne Egan Simmonds provided key assistance with loans and the catalog. This project, as with all art exhibitions, could not have been possible without the generosity of the lenders and cooperation of the thirteen artists.

Cheryl Washer
Project Director
SITES

98-0017(6M